BROADWAY PRESENTS

Audition | Musical Theatre Anthology

YOUNG FEMALE EDITION

CDs included

16–32 BAR EXCERPTS FROM STAGE & FILM

Includes Song Set-Up, Audition Tips, Vocal Style & Genre Indexes

Edited & Compiled by **Lisa DeSpain**

Alfred Music Publishing Co., Inc.
16320 Roscoe Blvd., Suite 100
P.O. Box 10003
Van Nuys, CA 91410-0003

ISBN10: 0-7390-6608-0
ISBN13: 978-0-7390-6608-9

alfred.com

Contents

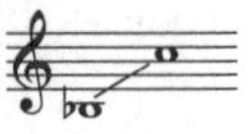

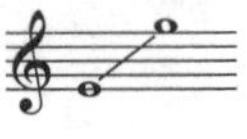

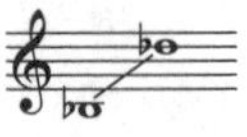

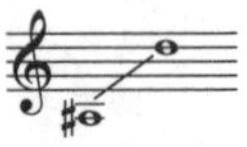

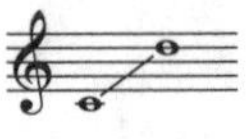

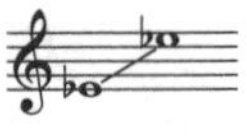

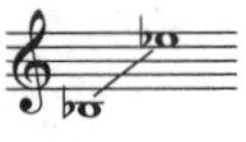

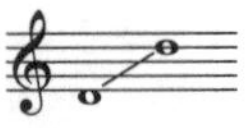

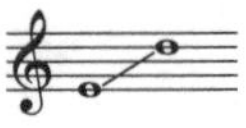

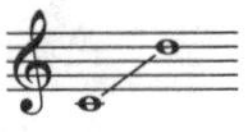

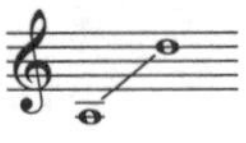

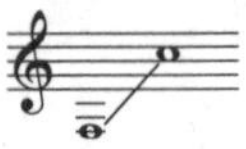

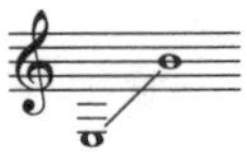

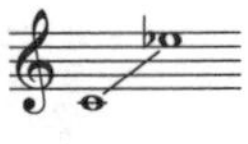

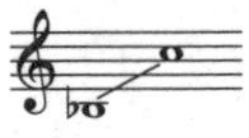

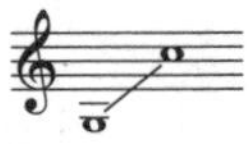

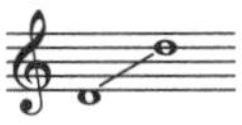

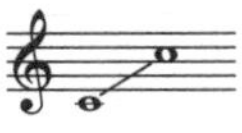

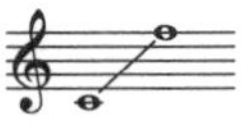

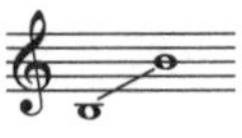

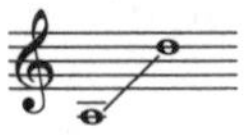

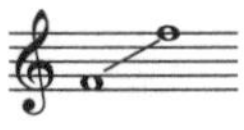

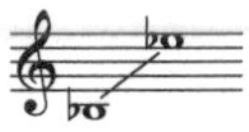

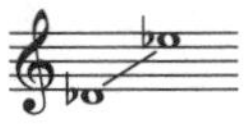

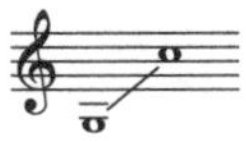

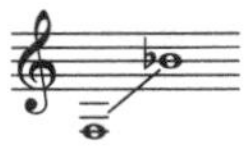

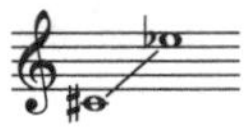

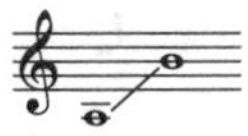

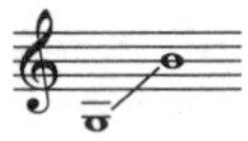

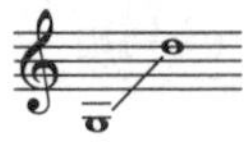

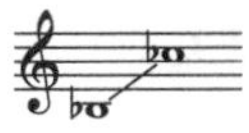

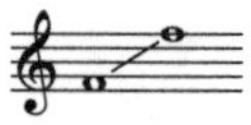

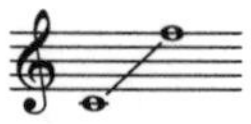

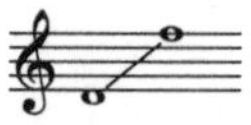

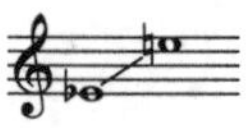

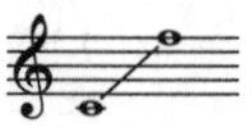

Introduction

Auditioning is a skill every musical theatre performer must learn. It is through auditioning that a director, casting agent, or teacher becomes familiar with your talents and makes the decision of how to cast you in a production. A musical theatre audition begins with the song.

Most auditions ask for a "16" or "32-bar cut," a shortened section of a song. In this small amount of time, is important to demonstrate both your vocal strengths and your ability to act a song. Every selection in this anthology is crafted to showcase these important skills. Although some selections presented are longer than 16 measures, they are of an appropriate length due to tempo. Longer cuts have optional starting points.

It is important to match the style of your song to the musical and vocal style of the production. Never sing a song from the production unless specifically asked, but choose a selection that sounds like it is from the same score.

Here are a few suggestions.

1. Determine the year the show or songs in the show were written and choose a song from around the same date. For example, if auditioning for *Singin' in the Rain*, which was written in 1928, the song, "Boy Wanted," composed in 1921 would be an excellent choice. Be careful with jukebox musicals, which are shows created using pre-existing songs. For example, although *Mamma Mia!* premiered on Broadway in 2001, the songs were written in the 1970s.
2. Sing a song written by the same composer but from a different show. For example, if auditioning for *My Fair Lady* composed by Alan Jay Lerner and Frederick Loewe, sing a song from *Camelot*.
3. If you have a specific character in mind, choose a song that demonstrates that character's attributes. Lois in *Kiss Me Kate* is a comedic role. Her big number is "Always True to You in My Fashion." The song "My Heart Belongs to Daddy" is also comedic and flirtatious. Lilli Vanessi, the female lead sings "So in Love," a dramatic ballad. Sing a dramatic ballad such as "My Funny Valentine."
4. Many musicals and characters are sung with specific vocal styles: legit, belt, mix or pop/contemporary. You want to match the singing style of the production in your audition song. A vocal teacher is the best resource to clarify these terms and coach you in the appropriate technique

I've included several indexes to help with choosing your song. I hope this book can be a guide and assist in making the musical decisions for your audition easier.

Break a leg!

Lisa DeSpain

Lisa DeSpain is a New York City based musical theater director, composer and audition accompanist. She serves on faculty at Professional Performing Arts School, New York City's premiere public school for teens training for and performing on Broadway.

Song Set Up

All For You
Seussical the Musical
Timid Gertrude McFuzz finally gains the courage to tell Horton the Elephant her true feelings after loyally following him through many difficult adventures.

All I Do is Dream of You
Singin' in the Rain
Kathy, a chorus girl, sings this production number at a Hollywood party where she sees Don Lockwood, a famous actor she rebuffed earlier that evening.

Always True to You in My Fashion
Kiss Me Kate
The fickle starlet Lois explains her weakness for flirting, yet reassures her sweetheart, Bill, that she loves him…in her own fashion.

And All That Jazz
Chicago
The opening number of the show, setting the world of murder, greed, corruption and violence in Chicago's jazz age.

Amayzing Mayzie
Seussical the Musical
The glamorous Mayzie tells how she became "amayzing" – by taking a pill to alter her appearance. She encourages plain Gertrude to become like her.

Anything Goes
Anything Goes
After madcap adventures and romantic mayhem, club singer Reno Sweeney sings that, in their world, "Anything Goes."

Anytime (I Am There)
Elegies
A mother sings to her child from beyond the grave, promising to be present everywhere in his life.

Aquarius
Hair
The opening number of the show setting the world of the 1960s anti-war, anti-establishment movement.

Astonishing
Little Women
Betrayed and confused by Laurie's marriage proposal, Jo March recommits to her dream of doing something astonishing with her life.

Be a Lion
The Wiz
Dorothy believes Cowardly Lion already has courage inside him. She encourages him to find it in himself.

Bewitched, Bothered and Bewildered
Pal Joey
Vera, a woman not interested in love, finally admits she has fallen for Joey.

The Boy Friend
The Boy Friend
The young female pupils of Madame Dubonnet's Finishing School have thoughts for one thing only… the boy friend.

The Boy Next Door
Meet Me in St. Louis
Shy young Esther admits she has fallen in love, but worries that her feelings are not returned.

Boy Wanted
My One and Only
During a press interview, swimming star Edith shares her thoughts and requirements for romance.

Caution to the Wind
Striking 12
Freezing to death, the little match girl lights her matches one at a time for warmth. In the flames, she sees her beloved and departed Grandmother beckoning to her. She decides to light all her matches.

Change
A New Brain
The homeless Lisa asks for more than just money. She truly asks for "change."

Crossword Puzzle
Starting Here, Starting Now
An intellectual, overbearing crossword puzzle geek can't figure out why her man left her.

Diamonds Are a Girl's Best Friend
Gentlemen Prefer Blondes
Lorelei, a gold digger and nightclub singer, performs her unapologetic anthem.

Doll on a Music Box
Chitty Chitty Bang Bang
Disguised as a life-size toy doll, Truly Scrumptious sings to distract the evil Baron Bombast while the children he has captured escape.

Don't Rain on My Parade
Funny Girl
Ziegfeld Follies comedy star Fanny Brice has fallen in love with the charismatic playboy Nick Arnstein. Ignoring the advice of her friends, Fanny follows Nick to Europe, determined to do things her way.

Even Though
I Love You Because
Although Austin is not the type of man Marcy is usually attracted to, she admits that she loves him.

Funny
My Favorite Year
K.C., a no-nonsense staff assistant, is in love with Benjy, a young comedy writer. However, she rebuffs his romantic advances, feeling inadequate—she's just not funny.

Funny Honey
Chicago
Roxie sings in honor of her husband, who initially takes the rap for Roxie's crime, then rats her out when he realizes her duplicity.

Get Happy
***Summer Stock* (film)**
Reluctant farm girl Jane steps into the leading lady role during a show's final production number.

Gimme, Gimme
Thoroughly Modern Millie
Millie finally realizes that what she wants is true love with Jimmy instead of glamour and wealth.

Good Morning
Singin' in the Rain
Don Lockwood's first talking picture is a disaster. Don and friends spend the night creating a plan to save the film. Suddenly the dawn looks brighter.

Good Morning Starshine
Hair
Sheila sings of the simple pleasures of life to temporarily ease Claude's turmoil over his impending Army draft.

Hangin' Around with You
Strike Up the Band (1930)
A frustrated girl questions her sweetheart's commitment.

Here's Where I Stand
***Camp* (film)**
Jenna has learned to love and accept herself. She asks her critical parents to do the same.

Hold On
Secret Garden
The young orphan, Mary, is to be sent away to boarding school. Martha, the housemaid, encourages Mary not to despair. Things may turn out better.

Home
The Wiz
Having discovered the power that lies within her, Dorothy wishes for home.

How Are Things in Glocca Morra?
Finian's Rainbow
Sharon, wishing to return to Ireland, tempts her father with visions of home.

How Could I Ever Know
The Secret Garden
Lily appears and apologizes to her husband, Archibald, for the pain her death has caused. She encourages him to move beyond his grief and live a happy life.

I Can Cook, Too
On the Town
Hoping to spend more time with the young sailor in her car, New York City cab driver Hildy brags of her special skills.

I Could Have Danced All Night
My Fair Lady
Having finally mastered Prof. Higgins' elocution lessons, Cockney flower seller Liza sings of her excitement.

I Get a Kick Out of You
Anything Goes
Reno reveals her feelings of attraction to Billy, hoping he will join her on board a ship sailing for England.

I Got Rhythm
Girl Crazy
Polly leads the townspeople in a song celebrating their new found joy and community pride.

I Had Myself a True Love
St. Louis Woman
Scorned by her former lover, Lila sings her version of their romantic life.

I Loved You Once in Silence
Camelot
Queen Guenevere finally speaks of her forbidden romantic feelings for the knight Sir Lancelot.

I Speak Six Languages
25th Annual Putnam County Spelling Bee
Tired of having to do everything perfectly, teen spelling sensation Marcy Park discovers the joy in just being normal.

I Think I May Want to Remember Today
Starting Here, Starting Now
A young woman celebrates falling in love.

I Want it Now
Willy Wonka and the Chocolate Factory
The spoiled Veruca demands a golden goose from Mr. Wonka and throws a tantrum when he refuses.

I Want to Go to Hollywood
Grand Hotel
Frieda, an aspiring actress, desperately believes that fame and fortune in Hollywood will solve her problems.

I Wish I Were in Love Again
Babes in Arms
The flirtatious Dolores sings about her sometimes-stormy sometimes-happy romance with Gus.

If You Hadn't, But You Did
Two on the Aisle
A woman tells her cheating sweetheart goodbye—and lists her reasons for murdering him.

I'm a Stranger Here Myself
One Touch of Venus
After being brought to life, the statue Venus, Goddess of Love, is rebuffed romantically. Confused, she questions the human custom of falling in love.

I'm Here
The Color Purple
The downtrodden Celie finally acknowledges a love and acceptance of herself.

I'm Not at All in Love
Pajama Game
Union representative Babe emphatically denies that she has romantic feelings for Sid, the new factory superintendent.

Is It Really Me?
110 in the Shade
Blooming under the affection of the drifter Starbuck, Lizzie begins to acknowledge her beauty.

It's a Perfect Relationship
Bells Are Ringing
Ella, a good-hearted telephone-answering operator has fallen in love with a man she knows only by his voice.

Let's Play a Love Scene
Fame: The Musical
Drama student Serena is tired of acting in scenes with Nick where she can't play her true emotions, so she offers a suggestion.

Light
Next to Normal
Closing number where everyone acknowledges that the journey of life is difficult, but can be lightened by love and honesty.

A Little Bit in Love
Wonderful Town
Eileen, a beautiful and charming small town girl, arrives in New York and instantly falls in love with all the local male residents.

A Little Brains, A Little Talent
Damn Yankees
The seductive Lola is enlisted by Applegate, the devil, to distract his latest victim. Lola brags of her particular skills with men.

Look to the Rainbow
Finian's Rainbow
Sharon explains her father's philosophy for happiness in life.

Love Who You Love (Adele's Reprise)
A Man of No Importance
The humble shop girl Adele expresses her love and friendship for Alfie, who has been shunned by the community for being gay.

Lovely
A Funny Thing Happened on the Way to the Forum
The clueless courtesan Philia may not be smart, but she has one important talent: being lovely.

Mama Who Bore Me
Spring Awakening
Wendla is confused by her changing body and new emotions. She wonders why her mother won't answer her questions.

Mama Who Bore Me (Reprise)
Spring Awakening
The young women are angry at their mothers' refusals to help them understand their new, womanly bodies.

Mamma Mia!
Mamma Mia!
Donna questions her turbulent emotions after seeing her three former boyfriends.

The Man I Love
Strike Up the Band (1927)
A young woman dreams of romance.

Mira
Carnival
Lili, an orphan, explains that she has come from the faraway town of Mira to find work with the carnival.

Much More
The Fantasticks
Luisa is young and in love, but dreams of an adventure-filled life.

The Music That Makes Me Dance
Funny Girl
Nick and Fanny have been separated for 18 months. On the evening of Nick's return, Fanny acknowledges the love she feels for him.

My Friend, the Dictionary
25th Annual Putnam County Spelling Bee
Spelling bee contestant Olive, lonely and ignored by her parents, sings of her constant companion and source of comfort.

My Funny Valentine
Babes in Arms
Billie sings of her unrequited love for the handsome Val.

My Heart Belongs to Daddy
Leave it to Me
A young siren sings her philosophy of love.

My Heart Stood Still
A Connecticut Yankee
Alice describes her feelings upon seeing her old flame, Martin.

The New Girl in Town
Hairspray: The Movie
Jealous of Tracy's popularity, especially with her boyfriend, the shallow and conniving Amber sings a not-so-subtle warning.

Not For the Life of Me
Thoroughly Modern Millie
Millie, a small town girl, arrives in New York City and is promptly mugged. When a stranger tells her to go back home, she refuses.

Notice Me Horton
Seussical the Musical
Plain Gertrude has grown a very long tail, hoping to impress Horton the Elephant. She pleads unsuccessfully for his attention.

Once Upon a Dream
Jekyll & Hyde
The affianced Emma, sensing Jekyll's changed nature, pleads for him to remember their love and promises not to abandon him.

Only Love
The Scarlet Pimpernel
The newly married Marguerite is confused as to why her husband, Percy, no longer loves her. She pleads for them to love again.

Out Here On My Own
Fame: The Movie
A young singer acknowledges that thoughts of those she loves keeps her from feeling lonely while trying to make her way in the world.

Over the Rainbow
The Wizard of Oz
Dorothy believes that the world beyond Kansas is magical, and she longs to see it.

Princess
A Man of No Importance
Feeling unworthy, Adele, a common shop girl, declines Alfie's offer to play the role of a princess in his theater production. But because of Alfie's belief, Adele's self-esteem grows and she eventually accepts the role.

Raunchy
110 in the Shade
Lizzie, a plain young woman without artifice, pokes fun of the flirtatious, glamorous girls in town and their ways to catch men.

Rhode Island is Famous for You
Inside U.S.A.
An admirer sings about the virtues of her beloved's home state.

Roxie
Chicago
Capitalizing on her sensational crime, the murderess Roxie dreams of stardom and celebrity.

The Sailor of My Dreams
Dames at Sea
An aspiring chorus girl named Ruby has fallen for Dick, a young sailor and aspiring songwriter.

Show Me
My Fair Lady
Fleeing Prof. Higgins' home, Eliza encounters Freddy who professes love with flowery words. She angrily turns on Freddy and demands action.

Shy
Once Upon a Mattress

Princess Winnifred hopes to marry Prince Dauntless. When the shy Dauntless does not step forward to present himself, Winnifred states that she understands, for she is shy, too.

The Simple Joys of Maidenhood
Camelot

Fearful of marriage to a man she does not know, Princess Guenevere escapes to the woods and prays for a return to maiden life.

Some Things Are Meant to Be
Little Women

Knowing Beth is gravely ill, sisters Jo and Beth March acknowledge both the beautiful and difficult aspects of life.

Someone to Watch Over Me
Oh Kay! (1926)

A young girl dreams of falling in love.

Somewhere That's Green
Little Shop of Horrors

Audrey harbors a secret dream of a simple life with someone nice like Seymour, but doesn't think she is worthy.

The Story Goes On
Baby

Lizzie, a pregnant young music student is profoundly moved by her baby's first kick.

Suddenly Seymour
Little Shop of Horrors

Downtrodden Audrey finally accepts that a nice boy like Seymour could actually love a girl like her.

Superboy and the Invisible Girl
Next to Normal

Natalie, a modern-day teenager, is fed up with feeling invisible, competing with her long-deceased brother for her mother's attention.

Take Me to the World
***Evening Primrose* (TV)**

Ella has lived her life confined inside a department store. When the outsider Charles arrives, she begs for escape.

There Won't Be Trumpets
Anyone Can Whistle

Nurse Fay wishes for a hero to save her town from corrupt politicians.

This Is All Very New to Me
Plain and Fancy

Hilda, a naïve Amish girl, meets the city slicker Dan and mistakes kindness for romantic overtures.

Times Like This
Lucky Stiff

Uncomfortable at a glamorous French nightclub, Universal Dog Home representative Annabel sings of happiness in much simpler joys.

The Trolley Song
Meet Me in St. Louis

Esther invites John to accompany her on a visit to the fairgrounds. John almost misses the trolley, but jumps on at the last minute, to Esther's delight.

Waiting For Life
Once on This Island

The peasant Ti Moune has fallen in love with Daniel, a boy from the upper class. She prays to the gods for answers to her purpose in life, hoping that Daniel will be a part of it.

When I Look at You
The Scarlet Pimpernel

Confiding in a friend, Marguerite expresses confusion at her husband's changed behavior and coldness toward her.

Whispering
Spring Awakening

Young, unmarried Wendla is pregnant, and her friends have also fallen victim to pain and suffering. Yet Wendla remains hopeful as she thinks about the child she is carrying.

Wouldn't It Be Loverly
My Fair Lady

Eliza, a poor flower seller, imagines what life would be like with a bit more comfort and wealth.

You Took Advantage of Me
Present Arms

A young woman puts up no resistance to falling in love, she already is.

Your Daddy's Son
Ragtime

Sarah, a poor, unmarried domestic servant, begs her infant son's forgiveness for her past deeds and tries to explain her actions.

Song Indexes

Vocal Styles

Some songs, especially early standards, may be sung with different vocal styles or in a combination of styles, depending on acting intent. These will be listed in more than one category.

LEGIT

All I Do is Dream of You
Bewitched, Bothered and Bewildered
The Boy Friend
The Boy Next Door
Boy Wanted
Doll on a Music Box
Hangin' Around with You
How Are Things in Glocca Morra?
How Could I Ever Know
I Could Have Danced All Night
I Had Myself a True Love
I Loved You Once in Silence
I Think I May Want to Remember Today
I Wish I Were in Love Again
I'm a Stranger Here Myself
Is It Really Me?
A Little Bit in Love
Look to the Rainbow
Lovely
The Man I Love
Mira
Much More
My Funny Valentine
My Heart Belongs to Daddy
My Heart Stood Still
Over the Rainbow
Rhode Island is Famous for You
The Sailor of My Dreams
Show Me
The Simple Joys of Maidenhood
Someone to Watch Over Me
Take Me to the World
This Is All Very New to Me
The Trolley Song
Wouldn't It Be Loverly
You Took Advantage of Me
Your Daddy's Son

BELT

All For You
All I Do is Dream of You
Always True to You in My Fashion
And All That Jazz
Amayzing Mayzie
Anything Goes
Aquarius
Astonishing
Be a Lion
Caution to the Wind
Change
Crossword Puzzle
Diamonds Are a Girl's Best Friend
Don't Rain on My Parade
Funny
Funny Honey
Get Happy
Gimme, Gimme
Good Morning
Good Morning Starshine
Hangin' Around with You
Hold On
Home
I Can Cook, Too
I Get a Kick Out of You
I Got Rhythm
I Speak Six Languages
I Think I May Want to Remember Today
I Want it Now
I Want to Go to Hollywood
I'm Here
I'm Not at All in Love
If You Hadn't, But You Did
It's a Perfect Relationship
A Little Brains, A Little Talent
Mama Who Bore Me (Reprise)
Mamma Mia!
The Music That Makes Me Dance
The New Girl in Town
Not For the Life of Me
Raunchy
Roxie
Shy
Somewhere That's Green

The Story Goes On
Suddenly Seymour
Superboy and the Invisible Girl
Take Me to the World
There Won't Be Trumpets
Times Like This
Waiting for Life

MIX

Anytime (I Am There)
Be a Lion
Even Though
Funny
Good Morning Starshine
Here's Where I Stand
Hold On
Home
Let's Play a Love Scene
Light
Love Who You Love (Adele's Reprise)
Mama Who Bore Me
Mamma Mia!
My Friend, the Dictionary
The New Girl in Town
Notice Me Horton
Once Upon a Dream
Only Love
Out Here On My Own
Princess
Rhode Island is Famous for You
Some Things Are Meant to Be
Superboy and the Invisible Girl
Times Like This
When I Look at You

Comedy/Dramatic

DRAMATIC

And All That Jazz
Anytime (I Am There)
Aquarius
Astonishing
Be a Lion
Bewitched, Bothered and Bewildered
The Boy Next Door
Caution to the Wind
Change
Doll on a Music Box
Don't Rain on My Parade
Even Though
Good Morning Starshine
Here's Where I Stand
Hold On
Home
How Are Things in Glocca Morra?
How Could I Ever Know
I Could Have Danced All Night
I Had Myself a True Love
I Loved You Once in Silence
I Think I May Want to Remember Today
I Want to Go to Hollywood
I'm Here
Is it Really Me?
Let's Play a Love Scene
Light
A Little Bit in Love
Look to the Rainbow
Love Who You Love (Adele's Reprise)
Mama Who Bore Me
Mama Who Bore Me (Reprise)
The Man I Love
Mira
Much More
The Music That Makes Me Dance
My Funny Valentine
My Heart Stood Still
Notice Me Horton
Once Upon a Dream
Only Love
Out Here On My Own
Over the Rainbow
Princess
Roxie
The Sailor of My Dreams
Show Me
The Simple Joys of Maidenhood
Some Things Are Meant to Be
Someone to Watch Over Me
The Story Goes On
Superboy and the Invisible Girl
Take Me to the World
There Won't Be Trumpets
Times Like This
Waiting for Life
When I Look at You
Whispering
Your Daddy's Son

COMEDIC

All for You
All I Do is Dream of You
Always True to You in My Fashion
Amayzing Mayzie
Anything Goes
The Boy Friend
Boy Wanted
Crossword Puzzle
Diamonds Are a Girl's Best Friend
Funny
Funny Honey
Get Happy
Gimme, Gimme
Good Morning
Hangin' Around with You
I Can Cook, Too
I Get a Kick Out of You
I Got Rhythm
I Speak Six Languages
I Wish I Were in Love Again
I Want it Now
I'm a Stranger Here Myself
I'm Not at All in Love
If You Hadn't, But You Did
It's a Perfect Relationship
A Little Bit in Love
A Little Brains, A Little Talent
Lovely
Mamma Mia!
My Friend, the Dictionary
My Heart Belongs to Daddy
The New Girl in Town
Not For the Life of Me
Raunchy
Rhode Island is Famous for You
Roxie
Shy
Somewhere That's Green
Suddenly Seymour
This Is All Very New to Me
Times Like This
The Trolley Song
Wouldn't It Be Loverly
You Took Advantage of Me

Historical Category

Standard, Golden Age, Contemporary, Pop/Rock

STANDARD

All I Do is Dream of You
Anything Goes
Bewitched, Bothered and Bewildered
Boy Wanted
Get Happy
Good Morning
Hangin' Around with You
I Get a Kick Out of You
I Got Rhythm
I Wish I Were in Love Again
If You Hadn't, But You Did
The Man I Love
My Funny Valentine
My Heart Belongs to Daddy
My Heart Stood Still
Rhode Island is Famous for You
Someone to Watch Over Me
You Took Advantage of Me

GOLDEN AGE

Always True to You in My Fashion
The Boy Friend
The Boy Next Door
Diamonds Are a Girl's Best Friend
Doll on a Music Box
Don't Rain on My Parade
How Are Things in Glocca Morra?
I Can Cook, Too
I Could Have Danced All Night
I Had Myself a True Love
I Loved You Once in Silence
I Want it Now
I'm a Stranger Here Myself
I'm Not at All in Love
Is it Really Me?
It's a Perfect Relationship
A Little Bit in Love
A Little Brains, A Little Talent
Look to the Rainbow
Lovely

Mira
Much More
The Music That Makes Me Dance
Over the Rainbow
Raunchy
The Sailor of My Dreams
Show Me
Shy
The Simple Joys of Maidenhood
Take Me to the World
There Won't Be Trumpets
This Is All Very New to Me
The Trolley Song
Wouldn't It Be Loverly

CONTEMPORARY

All For You
Amayzing Mayzie
And All That Jazz
Anytime (I Am There)
Astonishing
Be a Lion
Caution to the Wind
Change
Crossword Puzzle
Even Though
Funny
Funny Honey
Gimme, Gimme
Good Morning Starshine
Here's Where I Stand
Hold On
Home
How Could I Ever Know
I Speak Six Languages
I Want to Go to Hollywood
I Think I May Want to Remember Today
I'm Here
Let's Play a Love Scene
Light
Love Who You Love (Adele's Reprise)
Mama Who Bore Me
Mama Who Bore Me (Reprise)
Mamma Mia!
My Friend, the Dictionary
The New Girl in Town
Not For the Life of Me
Notice Me Horton
Once Upon a Dream
Only Love
Out Here On My Own
Princess
Roxie
Some Things Are Meant to Be
Somewhere That's Green
The Story Goes On
Suddenly Seymour
Superboy and the Invisible Girl
Times Like This
Waiting for Life
Whispering
Your Daddy's Son

POP/ROCK

Aquarius (60s)
Caution to the Wind (Pop)
Even Though (Pop)
Good Morning Starshine (60s)
Here's Where I Stand (R&B)
Home (Pop)
Let's Play a Love Scene (80s)
Light (Rock)
Mamma Mia! (70s)
The New Girl in Town (60s)
Superboy and the Invisible Girl (Rock)

Timeline

Songs are listed by the year they were composed. If used in a later production, the additional year is listed in parenthesis.

1921 Boy Wanted
My One and Only (1983)

1926 Someone to Watch Over Me
Oh Kay!

1927 The Man I Love
Strike Up the Band

1927 My Heart Stood Still
A Connecticut Yankee

1928 All I Do is Dream of You
Singin' in the Rain

1928 Good Morning
Singin' in the Rain

1928 You Took Advantage of Me
Present Arms

1930 Get Happy
Summer Stock (1950 film)

1930 Hangin' Around with You
Strike Up the Band

1930 I Got Rhythm
Girl Crazy

1934 Anything Goes
Anything Goes

1934 I Get a Kick Out of You
Anything Goes

1937 I Wish I Were in Love Again
Babes in Arms

1937 My Funny Valentine
Babes in Arms

1938 My Heart Belongs to Daddy
Leave it to Me

1939 Over the Rainbow
The Wizard of Oz

1940 Bewitched, Bothered and Bewildered
Pal Joey

1943 I'm a Stranger Here Myself
One Touch of Venus

1944 The Boy Next Door
Meet Me in St. Louis

1944 The Trolley Song
Meet Me in St. Louis

1944 I Can Cook, Too
On the Town

1946 I Had Myself a True Love
St. Louis Woman

1947 How Are Things in Glocca Morra?
Finian's Rainbow

1947 Look to the Rainbow
Finian's Rainbow

1948 Always True to You in My Fashion
Kiss Me Kate

1948 Rhode Island is Famous for You
Inside U.S.A.

1949 Diamonds Are a Girl's Best Friend
Gentlemen Prefer Blondes

1951 If You Hadn't, But You Did
Two on the Aisle

1953 A Little Bit in Love
Wonderful Town

1954 The Boy Friend
The Boy Friend (1920's parody)

1954 I'm Not at All in Love
Pajama Game

1955 A Little Brains, A Little Talent
Damn Yankees

1955 This Is All Very New to Me
Plain and Fancy

1956 It's a Perfect Relationship
Bells Are Ringing

1956 I Could Have Danced All Night
My Fair Lady

1956 Show Me
My Fair Lady

1956 Wouldn't It Be Loverly
My Fair Lady

1959 Shy
Once Upon a Mattress

1960 Much More
The Fantasticks

1961 Mira
Carnival

1962 Lovely
A Funny Thing Happened on the Way to the Forum

1963 Is It Really Me?
110 in the Shade

1963 Raunchy
110 in the Shade

1964 There Won't Be Trumpets
Anyone Can Whistle

1964 Don't Rain on My Parade
Funny Girl

1964 The Music That Makes Me Dance
Funny Girl

1966 The Sailor of My Dreams
Dames at Sea (1930s parody)

1966 Take Me to the World
Evening Primrose (TV)

1967 I Loved You Once in Silence
Camelot

1967 The Simple Joys of Maidenhood
Camelot

1968 Doll on a Music Box
Chitty Chitty Bang Bang

1968 Aquarius
Hair

1968 Good Morning Starshine
Hair

1971 I Want it Now
Willy Wonka and the Chocolate Factory

1975 And All That Jazz
Chicago

1975 Funny Honey
Chicago

1975 Roxie
Chicago

1975 Mamma Mia!
Mamma Mia! (2001 Broadway)

1975 Be a Lion
The Wiz

1975 Home
The Wiz

1977 Crossword Puzzle
Starting Here, Starting Now

1977 I Think I May Want to Remember Today
Starting Here, Starting Now

1980 Out Here On My Own
Fame: The Movie

1982 Somewhere That's Green
Little Shop of Horrors

1982 Suddenly Seymour
Little Shop of Horrors

1983 The Story Goes On
Baby

1988 Let's Play a Love Scene
Fame: The Musical

1988 Times Like This
Lucky Stiff

1989 I Want to Go to Hollywood
Grand Hotel

1990 Waiting for Life
Once on This Island

1991 Hold On
Secret Garden

1991 How Could I Ever Know
The Secret Garden

1993 Funny
My Favorite Year

1997 Once Upon a Dream
Jekyll & Hyde

1997 Only Love
Scarlet Pimpernel

1997 When I Look at You
Scarlet Pimpernel

1998 Change
A New Brain

1998 Your Daddy's Son
Ragtime

2000 All For You
Seussical the Musical

2000 Amayzing Mayzie
Seussical the Musical

2000 Notice Me Horton
Seussical the Musical

2002 Love Who You Love (Adele's Reprise)
A Man of No Importance

2002 Princess
A Man of No Importance

2002 Gimme, Gimme
Thoroughly Modern Millie

2002 Not For the Life of Me
Thoroughly Modern Millie

2003 Anytime (I Am There)
Elegies

2003 Here's Where I Stand
Camp (film)

2004 Caution to the Wind
Striking 12

2005 I Speak Six Languages
25th Annual Putnam County Spelling Bee

2005 My Friend, the Dictionary
25th Annual Putnam County Spelling Bee

2005 I'm Here
The Color Purple

2005 Astonishing
Little Women

2005 Some Things Are Meant to Be
Little Women

2006 Even Though
I Love You Because

2006 Mama Who Bore Me
Spring Awakening

2006 Mama Who Bore Me (Reprise)
Spring Awakening

2006 Whispering
Spring Awakening

2007 The New Girl in Town
Hairspray (film)

2009 Light
Next to Normal

2009 Superboy and the Invisible Girl
Next to Normal

The Songs

ALL FOR YOU

(from "Seussical the Musical")

Lyrics by
LYNN AHRENS

Music by
STEPHEN FLAHERTY

CD/TRACK 1/1

B+
Cm/B♭
Am7(♭5)
D
Gm
stag-gered on one for you.
Now here I am, the
E♭m/G♭
B♭/F
Em7(♭5)
worse for wear, and here you are. I'm here! You're there! And
(Spoken:)
"Oh, yes. And Horton, one more thing..."
Cm7
C/D
D7
Gm
poco rit.
E♭m/G♭
p dolce
may - be now you'll know I care for you!
It
poco rit.
sub.
p
B♭/F
Gm7
F7sus/C
F
B♭
took me se - ven weeks.. but I found your clo - ver too.
p colla voce
dolce
pp

ALL I DO IS DREAM OF YOU

(from "Singin' in the Rain")

Words by
ARTHUR FREED

Music by
NACIO HERB BROWN

19
F7
Cm7
F7sus
B♭
Cm7
F7
au - tumn, and spring. And were there more than twen - ty - four hours a day,
sfz
24
Cm7
F
Cm7
F7
B♭
they'd be spent in sweet con - tent dream - ing a - way. When
sfz
29
B♭7
B♭7(♯5)
E♭
E♭m6
skies are grey, when skies are blue, morn - ing, noon, and night-time too,
33
B♭
F7
B♭
all I do the whole day through is dream of you.
sfz

ALWAYS TRUE TO YOU IN MY FASHION

(from "Kiss Me Kate")

Words and Music by
COLE PORTER

B9 E F♯m/E E A/E E9 A/C♯ A+/C♯ D
Tex is here to stay! But I'm al - ways true to you,
Bm7 A♭/C A/C♯ A13 Dm6 Bm7(♭5) Dm/F
darlin' in my fash - ion. Yes, I'm
A/E A+/E A6/E A7/E B13 Bm9/E
al - ways true to you, dar - lin' in my
A A/C♯ D6 D6/F♯ E E♭dim D B♭7(♭9) A7
way!

AMAYZING MAYZIE

(from "Seussical the Musical")

Lyrics by
LYNN AHRENS

Music by
STEPHEN FLAHERTY

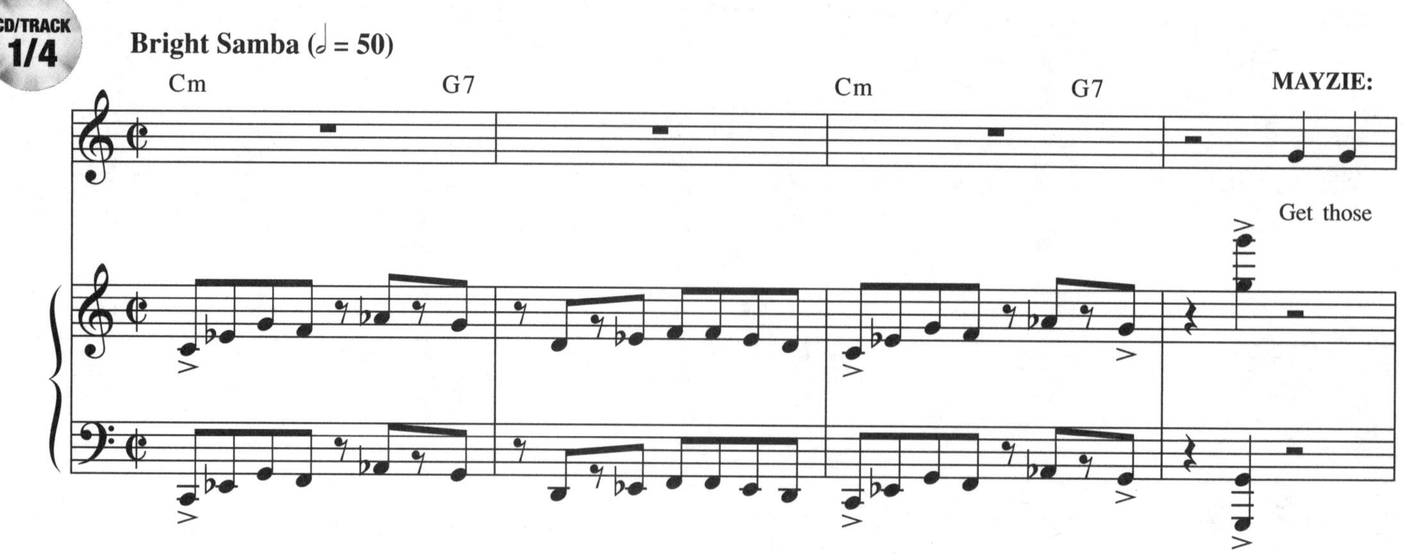

12
G7
C
And
you
can
be
a
-
may
-
zing...
sffz
17
D♭/G
D/G
E♭/G
G7
al
-
most
as
a
-
may
-
zing
as
sfz
21
Cm
G7
Cm
G7
me!!!!
25
Cm
G7
C(no3rd)
Zip!!
sfz

AND ALL THAT JAZZ
(from "Chicago")
Lyrics by
FRED EBB
Music by
JOHN KANDER
CD/TRACK
1/5
Moderately (♩ = 132)
B♭6
VELMA:
Oh, ___ you're gon - na see your She - ba shim - my shake, - And all that jazz! —
F+
B♭6
Oh, ___ I'm gon - na shim - my till my gar - ters break, - And all that jazz! —
F7
Show ___ me where to park my gir - dle.

13
G♭7
B♭
B♭/A
Fm6/A♭
G7
Oh, my moth-er's blood-'d cur-dle if she'd hear her ba-by's queer for
17
G♭7
F7
B♭
B♭/A
B♭/A♭
all that jazz!
No, I'm no one's wife but oh, I
sim.
23
G7
Cm7
Cm7/F
love my life and all that
28
B♭
B♭/A♭
E♭/G
E♭m/G♭
B♭/F
B♭
jazz!
That jazz!

ANYTHING GOES

(from "Anything Goes")

Words and Music by
COLE PORTER

16
Bm/A
G♯dim7
D/A
E♭/A
E7/D
Dm7
D+7
G
D+
prize to - day, are just sil - ly gig - o - los:
So, though I'm not a
f
20
G
G/F♯
G/E
Dm7
G7
C6
great ro - manc - er, I know that I'm bound to an - swer when you pro - pose,
24
Am7
Cm6
G
Cm
ad lib.
3
a tempo
an - y - thing goes.
An - y - thing goes!
ad lib.
a tempo
29
G
G/F
C/E
Cm/E♭
E♭/D
E♭m/D
G
ff

ANYTIME (I AM THERE)

(from "Elegies")

Words and Music by
WILLIAM FINN

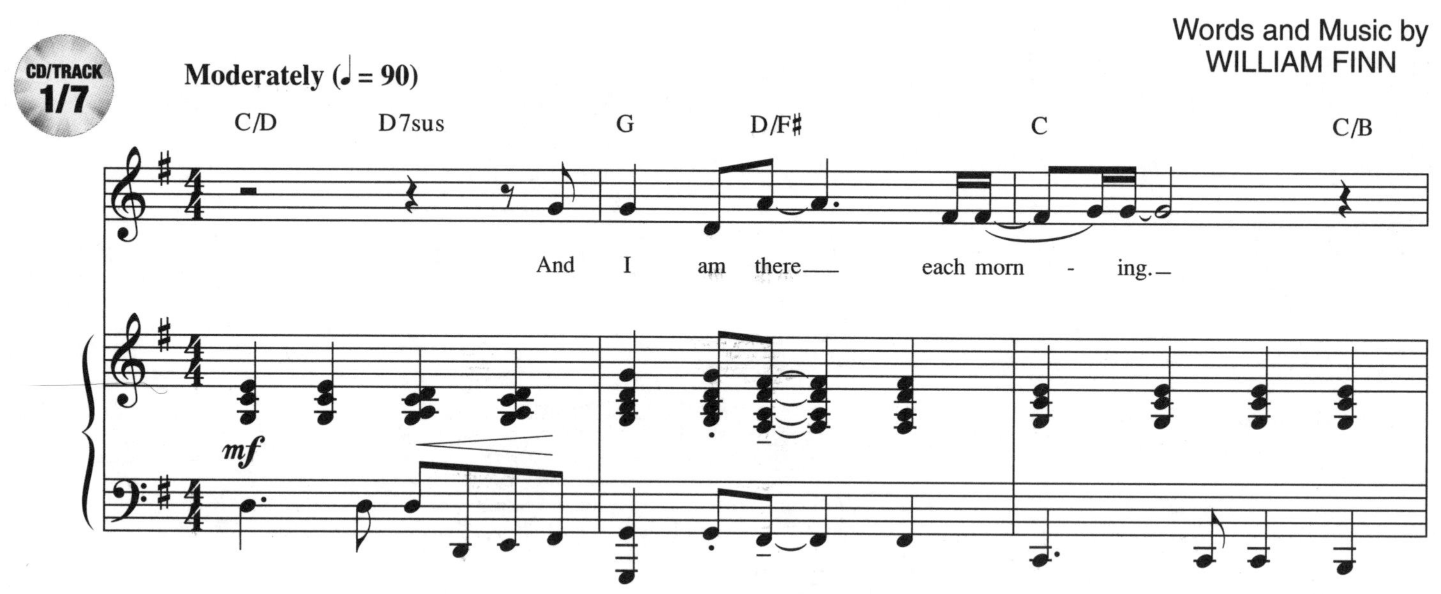

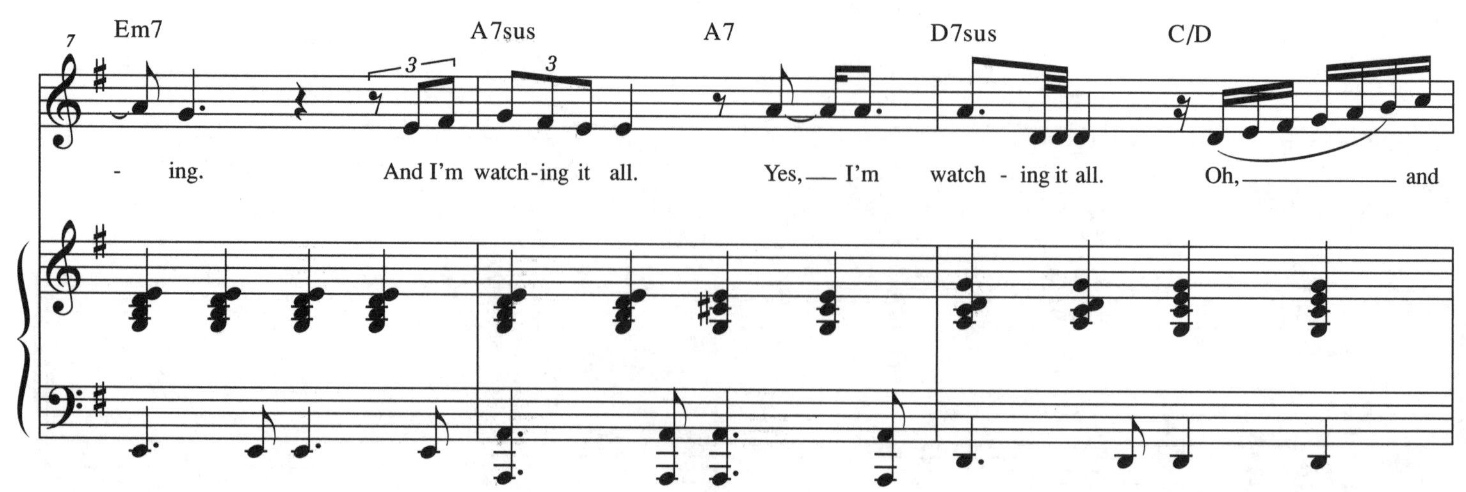

10
G D/F♯ C C/B Am7 D9
I am there in mu - sic. I am there in
13
G F/G G C B7 Em7 A7
sky. I don't know why this thing did hap - pen but this much is clear,
16
Am7/D D9 Am7/D D9 B7/D♯ Em D♯+ G/D A7/C♯
any-time or an-y where, I am there. I am there. I am there. I am
20
D7sus B♭/D Am7 D7sus B♭/D Am/D G(add9) C(add9)/G G(add9)
rit. freely
there. I am there.
freely
rit.
mp

AQUARIUS

(from "Hair")

Lyrics by
JAMES RADO and
GEROME RAGNI

Music by
GALT MACDERMOT

CD/TRACK 1/8

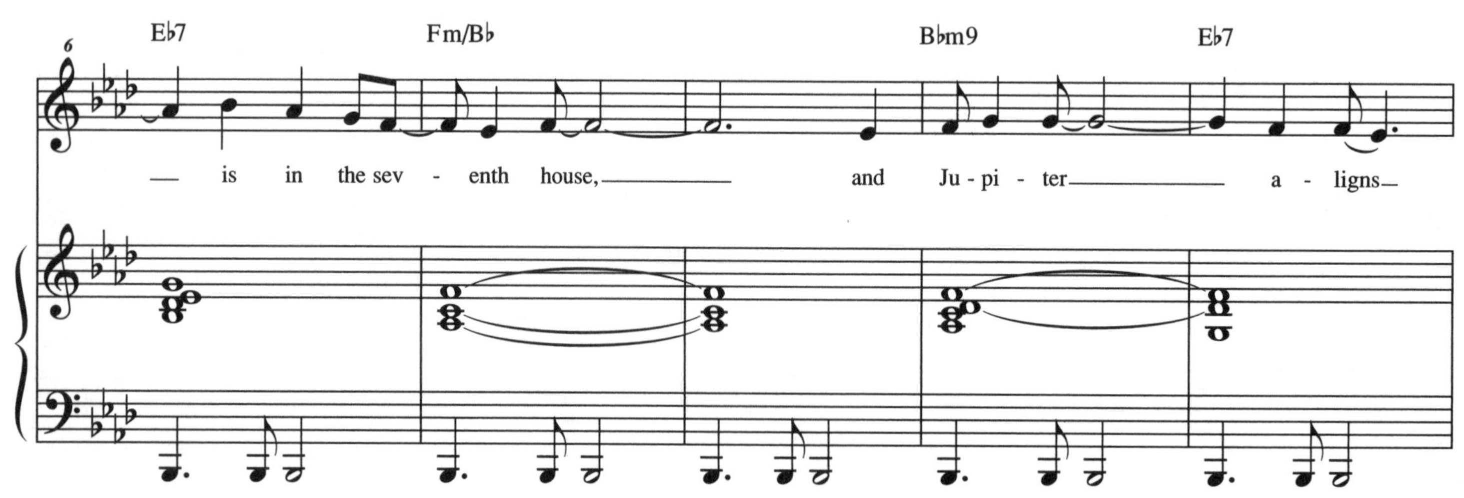

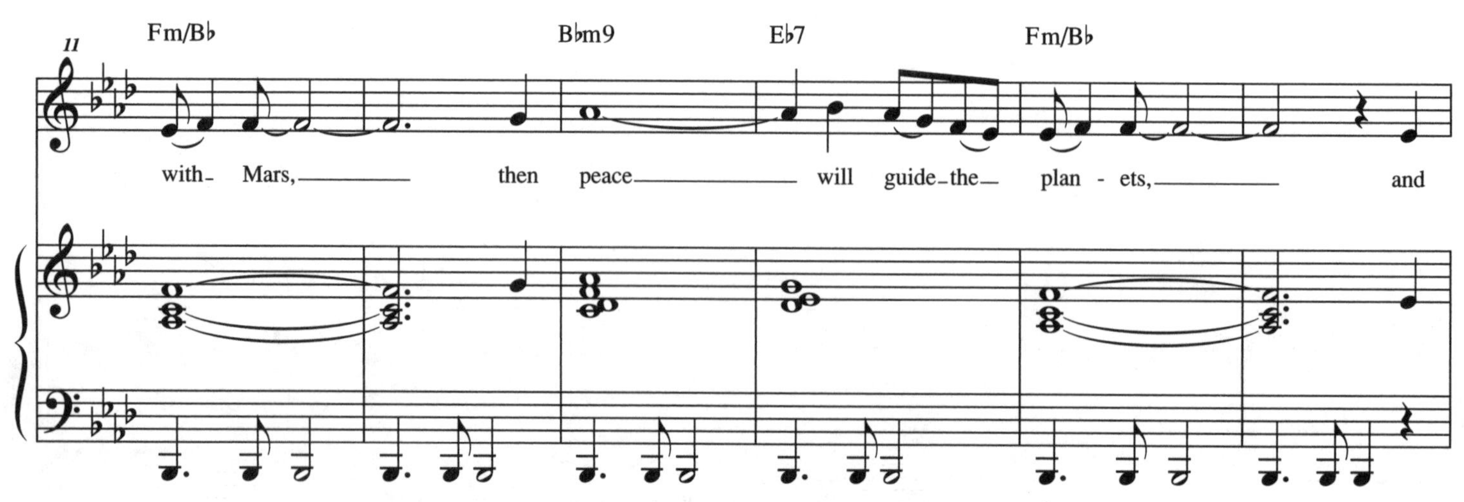

D♭ E♭7 A♭
mf
love will steer the stars. This is the dawn - ing of the
cresc.
G♭ B♭m
age of A - quar - i - us, age of A - quar - i - us.
mf
E♭
A - quar - i - us. A -
B♭m
1. 2.
quar - i - us. A -

ASTONISHING
(from "Little Women")

Lyrics by
MINDI DICKSTEIN

Music by
JASON HOWLAND

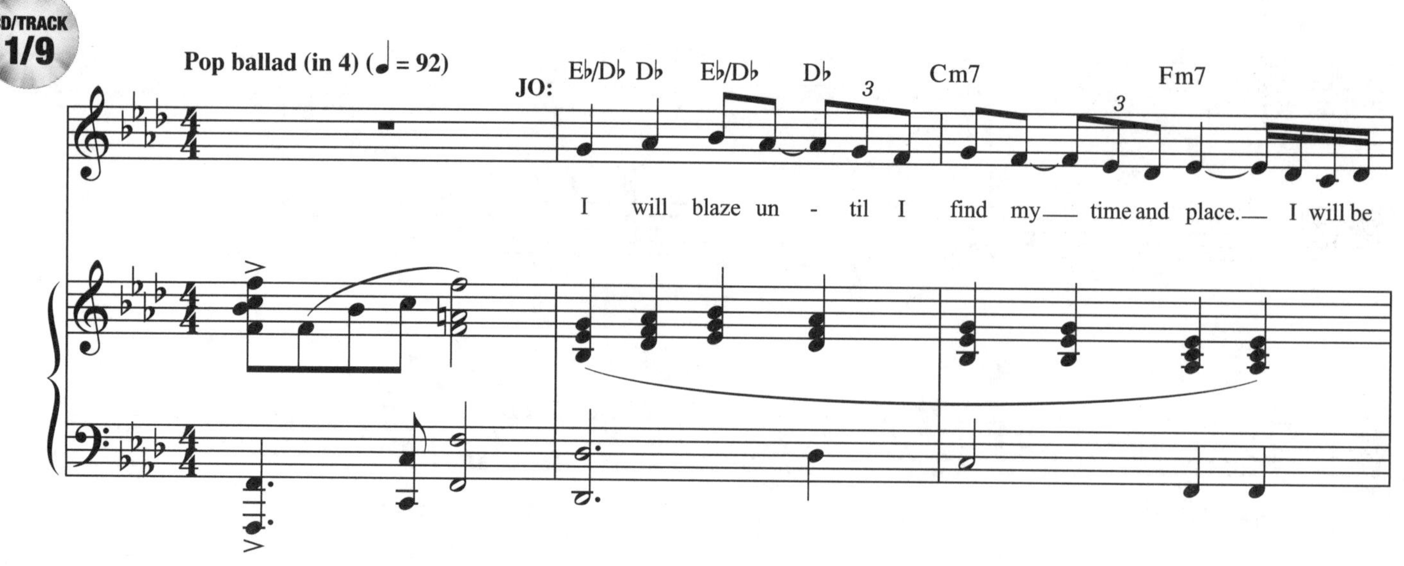

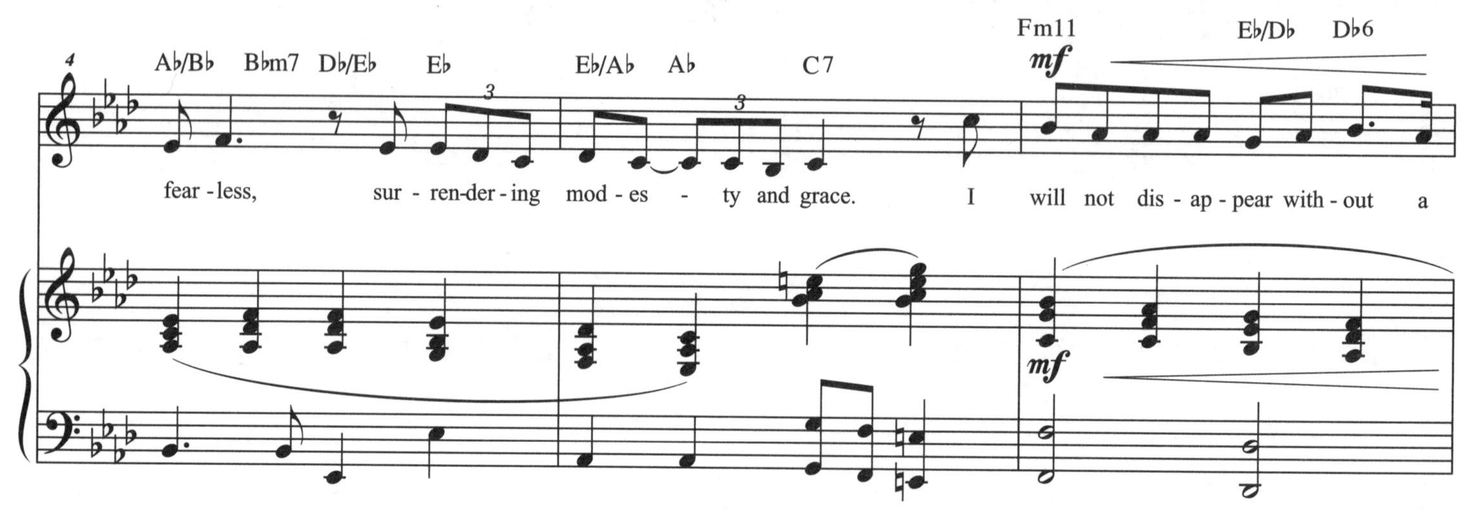

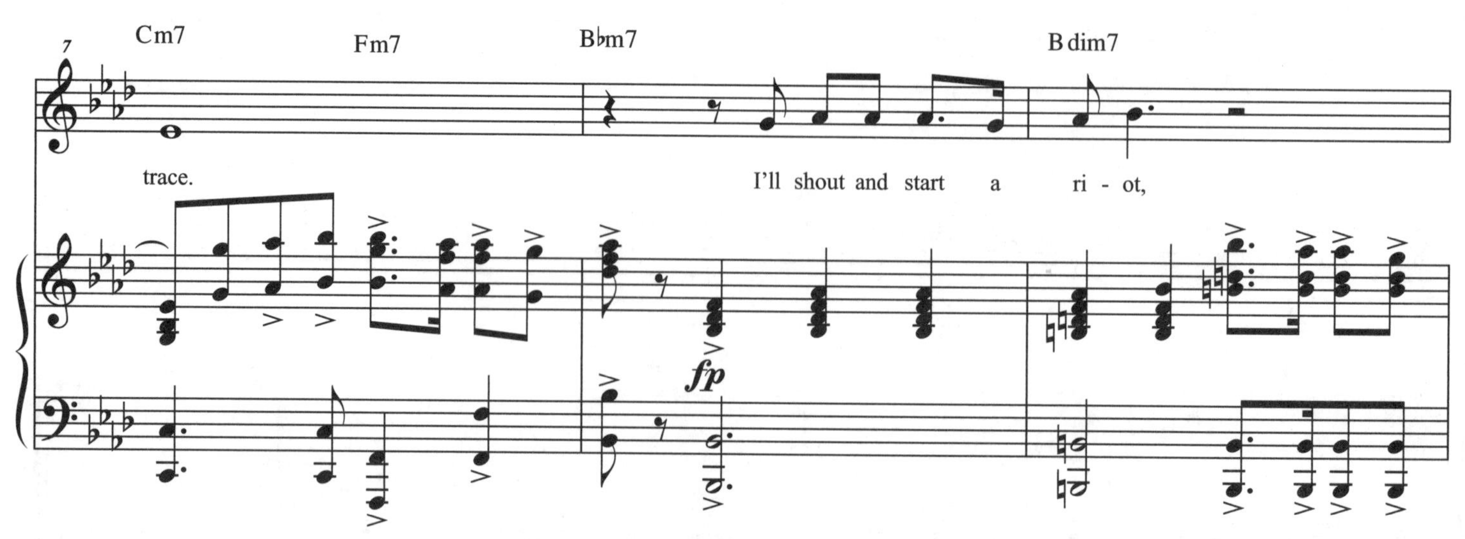

10
Ab/C
Fm11
Bbm7
Ab/C
be an-y-thing- but qui-et. Chris-to-pher Co-lum-bus, I'll be a-
13
Db6/9
Ab/Gb Gb
Gbmaj9
ston-ish-ing. A-ston-ish-ing, A-
16
Ab/Eb
molto rit.
E
Gb/Db
ston-ish-ing at last.
molto rit.
19
G/B
Amaj7
N.C.
Ab

BE A LION
(from "The Wiz")

Words and Music by
CHARLIE SMALLS

CD/TRACK 1/10

Waltz ballad, light swing (♩ = 76)

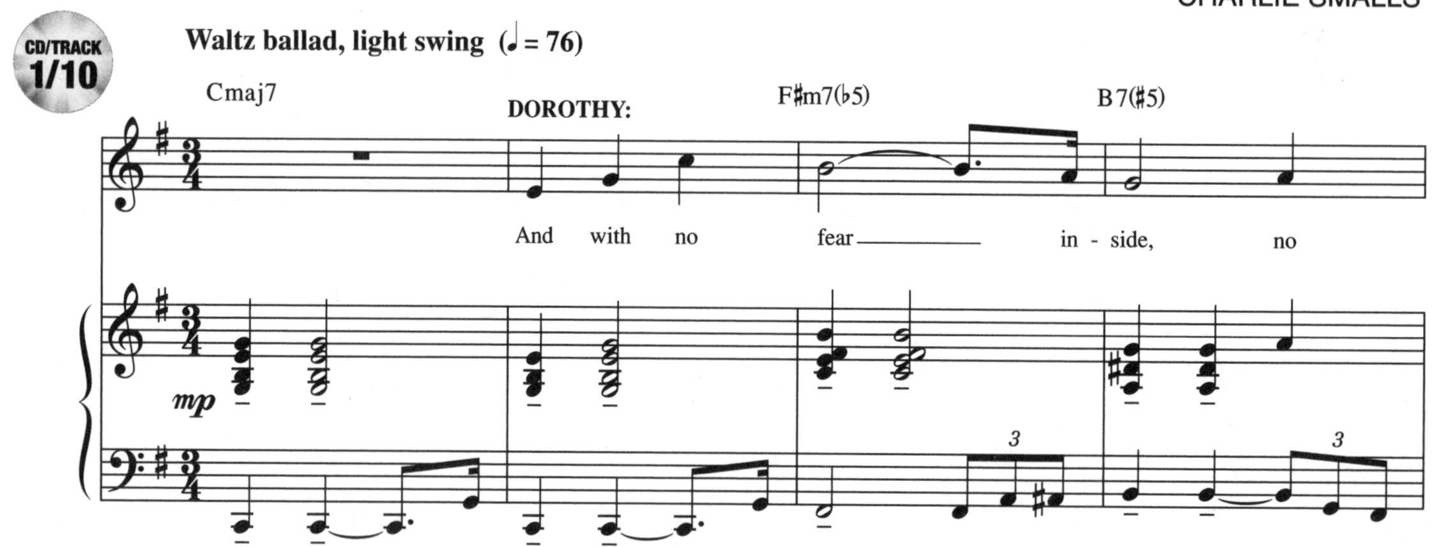

15
C/D
G/D
C/D
all. If on cour - age you must call, then
20
C
Bsus
B+
Em
just keep on try - in' and try - in' and try - in'.
3
24
E7
G/A
A9
C/D
You're a li - on in your own way,
f
3
28
D7sus/G
G
be a li - on!

BEWITCHED, BOTHERED and BEWILDERED

(from "Pal Joey")

Words by
LORENZ HART

Music by
RICHARD RODGERS

10
Dm7
G7
C6
Dm7
me. I'll sing to him, each Spring to him, and
13
C/E
C+/E
F
D dim7
C/E
D7
long for the day when I'll cling to him. Be - witched, both - ered and be -
16
G7
C
F
C
wil - dered am I.
8va

THE BOY FRIEND

(from "The Boy Friend")

Words and Music by
SANDY WILSON

CD/TRACK 1/12

13 C
f
C♯dim7
Dm
D♯dim7
C/E
C+/E
F
Fm
We sigh— for him, and cry— for him, and we would glad - ly die— for him,
17 C/E
E♭dim7
Dm7
G+9
C
Dm7
G9sus G7(♭9 ♯5)
that cer - tain thing called the Boy Friend.—
21 C
C♯dim7
Dm
D♯dim7
C/E
C+/E
F
Fm
We're blue— with - out, can't do— with - out, our dreams just won't come true— with - out
25 C/E
C+/E
Fmaj7
G7(♭9)
Cmaj9
C6
that cer - tain thing called the Boy Friend.
sfz

THE BOY NEXT DOOR

(from "Meet Me in St. Louis")

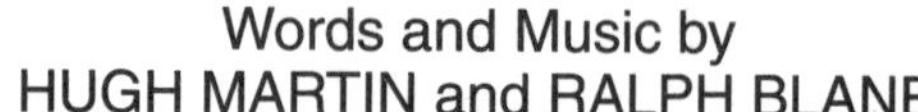

CD/TRACK 1/13

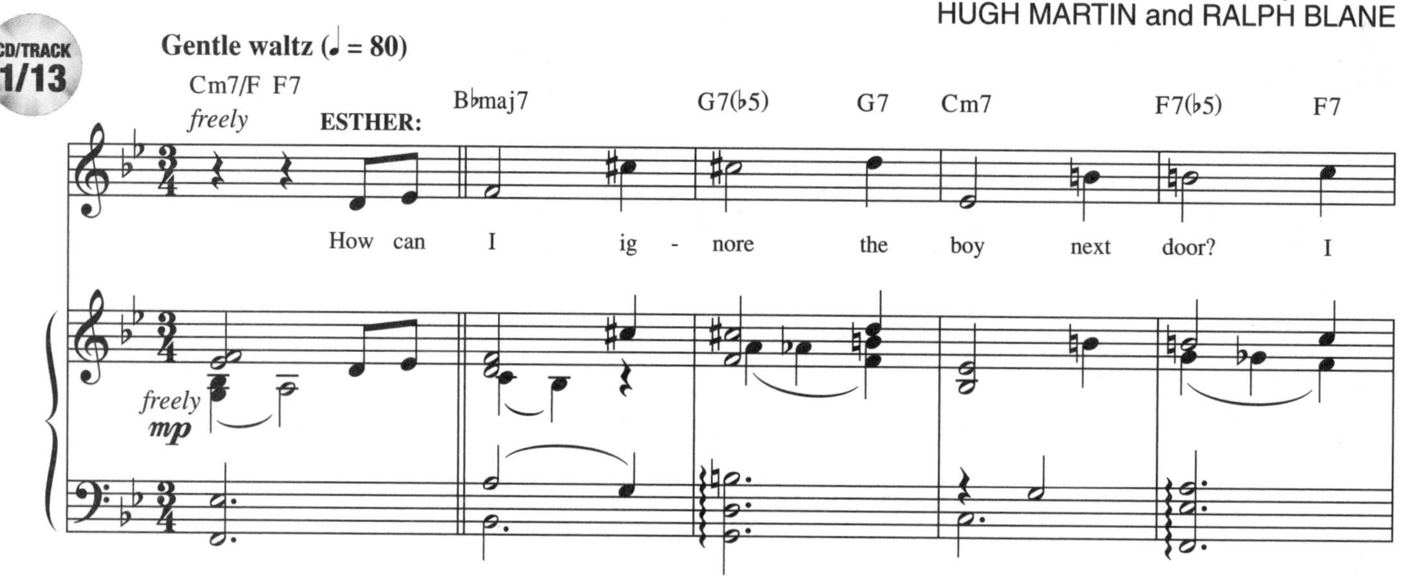

15
A7alt A7(♯9) Dm7 D♭dim7 Cm7 F7 B♭maj7
sees me glance his way. And though I'm heart -
19
G7(♭5) G7 Cm7 F7(♭5) F7 B♭maj7 Gm7
sore the boy next door, af - fec - tion for me won't dis -
24
C9 C7(♭5) B♭6/F A7/F B♭6/F Cm9
p
colla voce
play. I just a - dore him, so I can't ig -
p colla voce
29
D/C Cm7 B♭m7 F7 B♭6 Cm7 F7 B♭6
rit.
nore him, the boy next door.
rit.

BOY WANTED

(from "My One and Only")

Lyrics by
ARTHUR FRANCIS

Music by
GEORGE GERSHWIN

CD/TRACK 1/14

Moderato (𝅗𝅥 = 92–100)

EDITH:

mf

A7 D Em7 A7

He must be ten - der and true.

5 D6/9 Em7 A7 D D7

And he must know how to woo.

9 Gmaj7 Gm Em7(♭5) D(add9)/A

I know we'll get ac - quaint - ed might - y soon,

13 D Em Em7/D A9/C♯ A9

out in a gar - den 'neath a har - vest moon:

17
Dmaj7
C♯m7(♭5)
F♯7
and if he proves to be the right lit - tle
21
Bm
E9
A7
Adim7
lad - die,
I'll make him glad he
24
A9
D
B♭+
D
an - swered my "ad."

CAUTION TO THE WIND

(from "Striking 12")

Words and Music by
BRENDAN MILBURN,
VALERIE VIGODA
and RACHEL SHEINKIN

CD/TRACK 1/15

Medium groove with strong backbeat (♩ = 144)

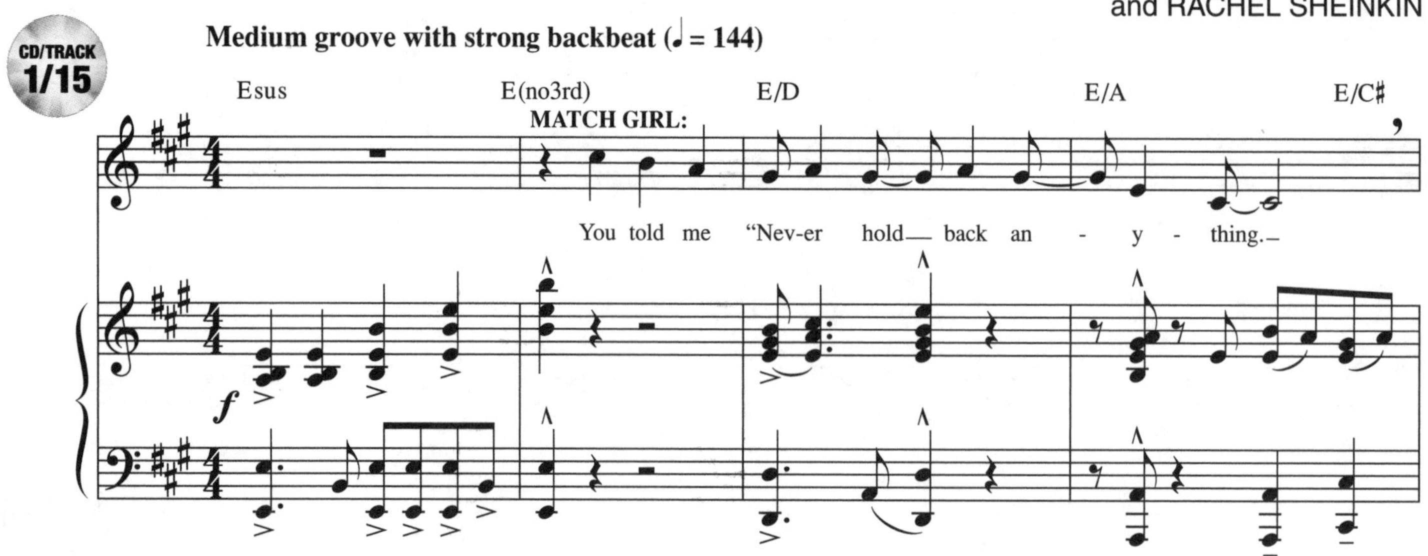

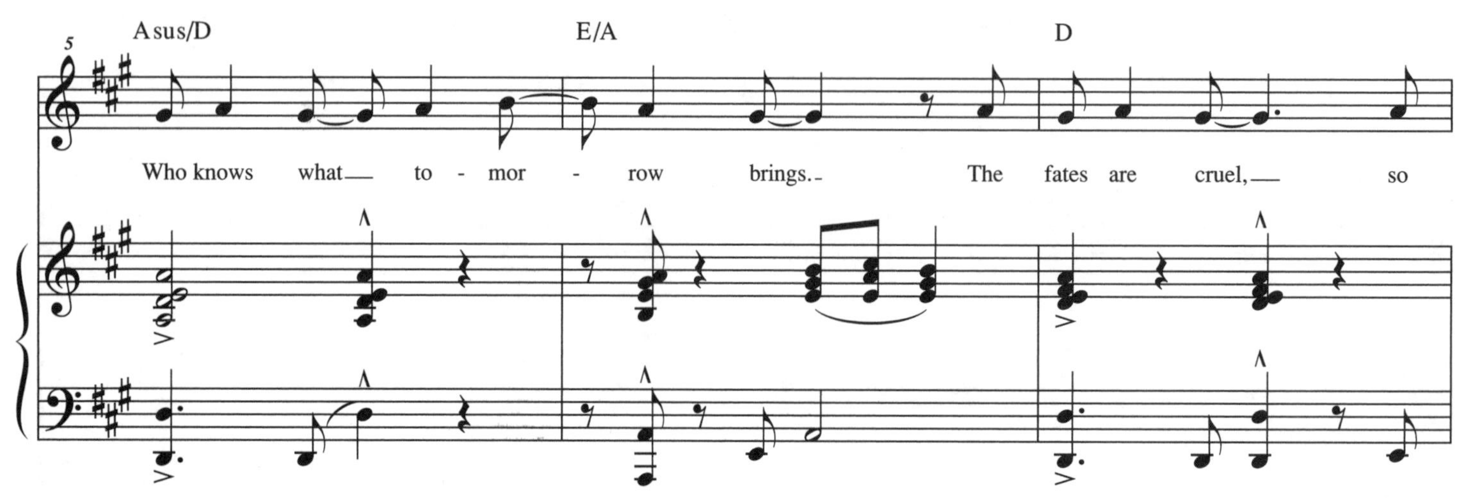

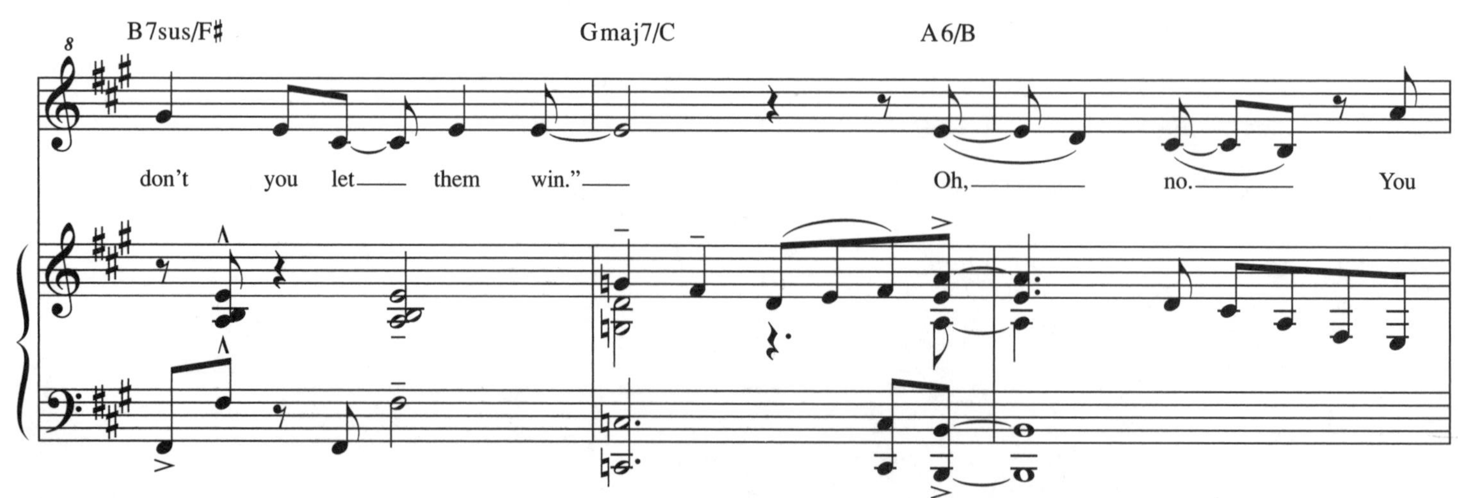

11
Asus/D
E/A
Asus/D
lived your life just like a flame that burned out fast, but seared
14
E/A
E/C♯
E(add4)/D
B7sus/F♯
Gmaj7/C
Bm7
your name a - cross my heart and ev - 'ry - where you'd been. Cau -
18
Misterioso
Csus/F
Gsus/C
Dsus
- tion to the wind. Burn my match - es to the end.
p
22
D
Csus/F
Gsus/C
D
Em
D/F♯
Throw - ing cau - tion to the wind.

CHANGE

(from "A New Brain")

Words and Music by
WILLIAM FINN

20
Gm7 Gm7/F B♭/E♭ B♭(add9)/D D7 D7/F♯ Gm7
- tion. I'm not ask - ing for par - a - dise.
25
Gm6 E♭6
All I'm ask - ing for
30
Fsus N.C. B♭ A♭maj7/F B♭ A♭maj7/F B♭ A♭maj7/F
is change!
ff
36
F7sus B♭
sub. p
cresc.
ff
8va

CROSSWORD PUZZLE

(from "Starting Here, Starting Now")

Words by
RICHARD MALTBY, JR.

Music by
DAVID SHIRE

14 C6 C9 F6 Fm6 C/E Am7 D9
doubt. All at once Heck-y's jump - ing and scream-ing and yell-ing. I tell you, the four let-ter words that came
18 G C(add9) Dm7
"Out. Pre-fix" that means "Pro." P - R - O. Bo-de - o-do. Starts you feel-ing as if hav-ing
23 Cmaj7/E Am11 Dm7 E7sus/B E7 Am Am/G F♯m7(♭5) Fm7
brains or in-tel-li-gence was one of the world's worst crimes. And the sen-tence is do-ing the
27 C/E Am7 Dm7 G9sus N.C. C/F♯ N.C.
cross-word puz - zle in the Sun-day Times!
8va

DIAMONDS ARE A GIRL'S BEST FRIEND

(from "Gentlemen Prefer Blondes")

Words by
LEO ROBIN

Music by
JULE STYNE

CD/TRACK 1/18

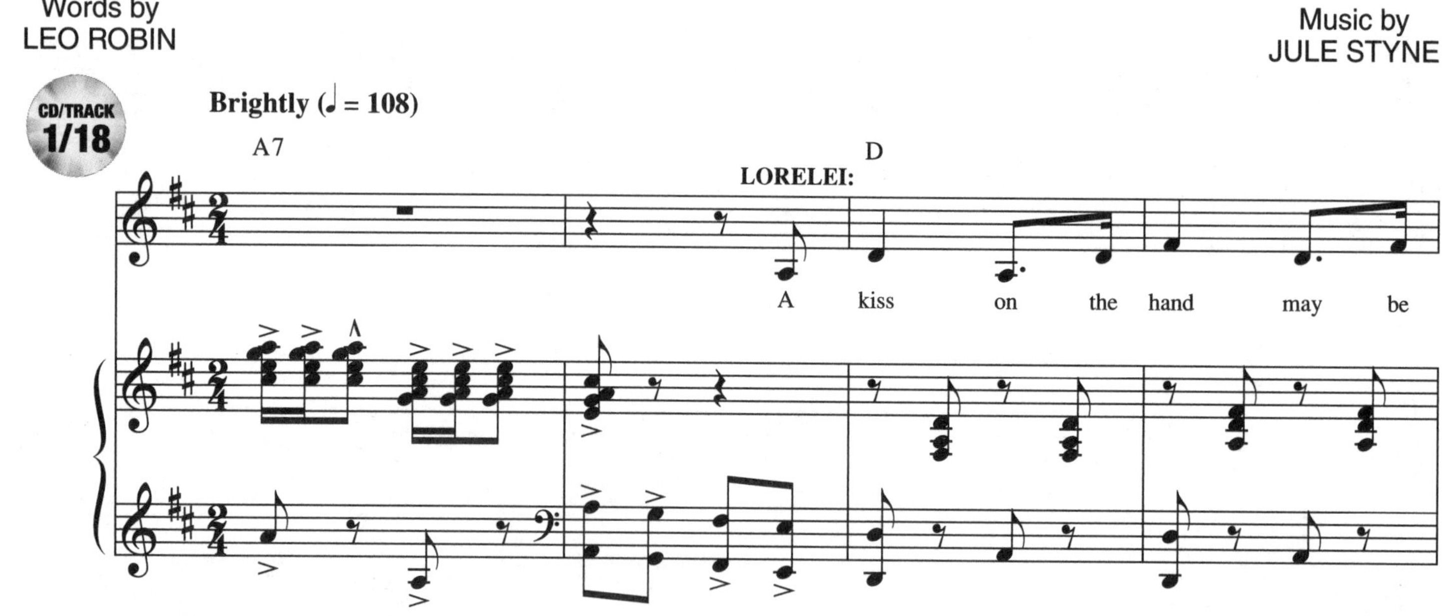

15
E7 D/F♯ Gdim E7/G♯ A7sus Em9 A9 Am/D Ddim7
hum - ble flat or help you at the Au - to - mat. Men grow
20
Am/D D7 G Gdim7 G D/F♯ Bm E7
cold as girls grow old and we all lose our charms in the
25
A7 Gmaj7/A A7 D D/C♯ Am6/C
end. But square - cut or pear - shape, these rocks don't lose
30
F♯m7 B7 Em7 A7 D Em/D Fm/D D
their shape. Dia - monds are a girl's best friend!

DOLL ON A MUSIC BOX

(from "Chitty Chitty Bang Bang")

Words and Music by
RICHARD M. SHERMAN
and
ROBERT B. SHERMAN

CD/TRACK 1/19

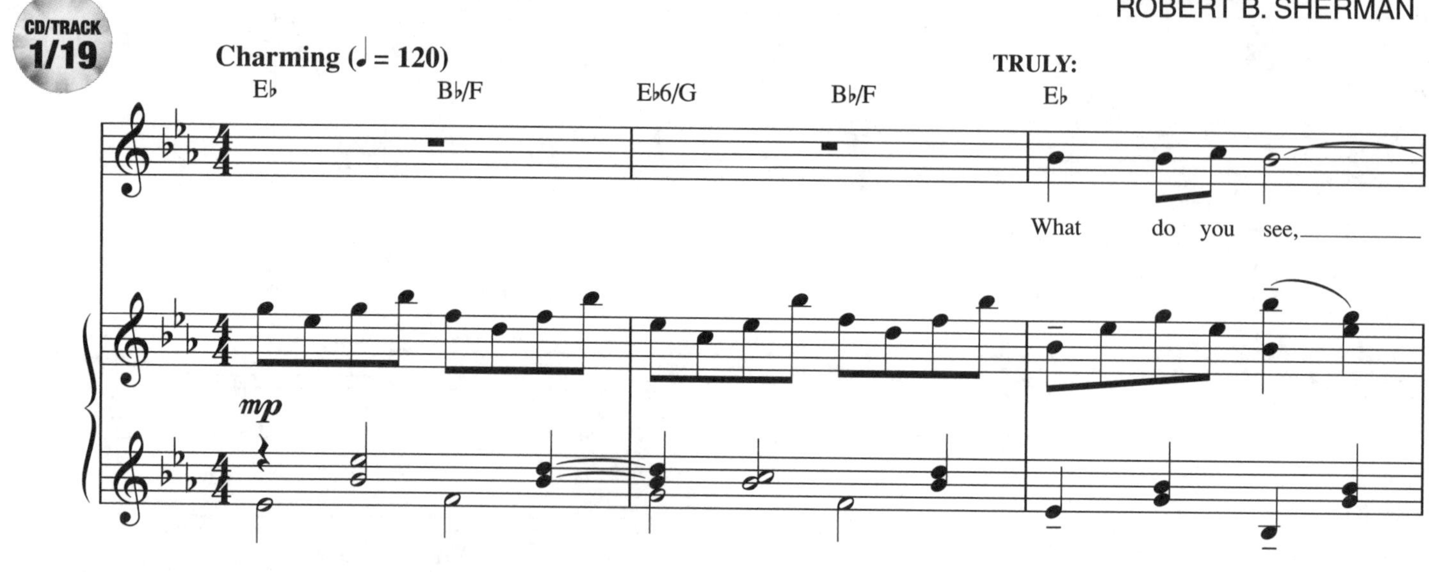

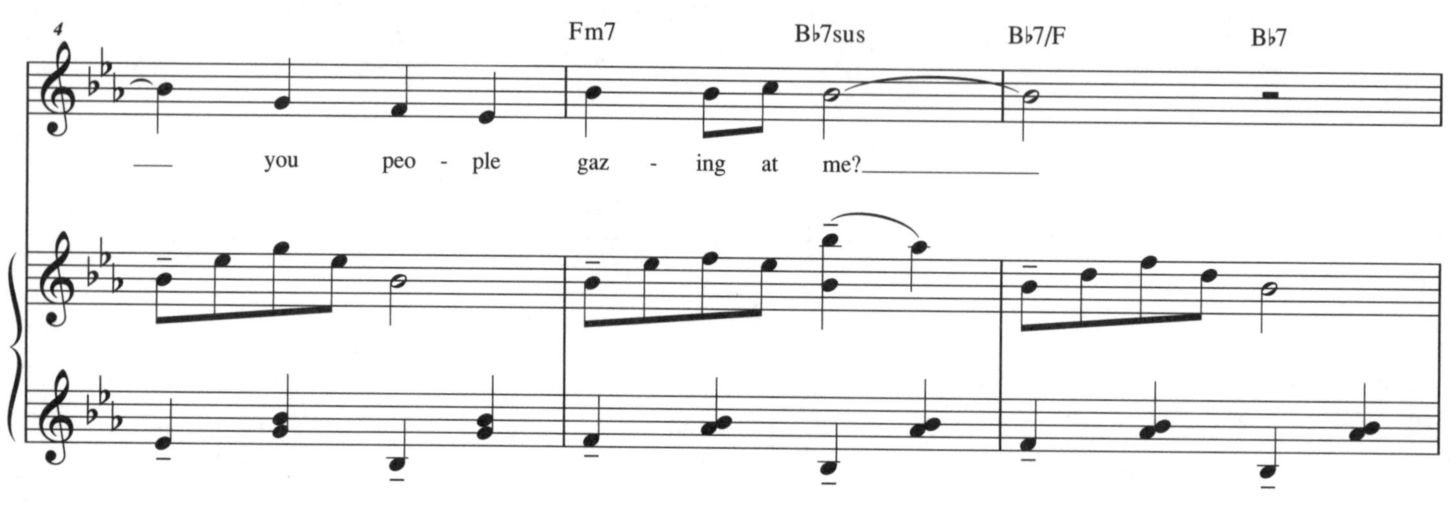

10
C7(♭9) Dm7(♭5)
C7/E
Fm
B♭7
Yearn - ing,
13
Gm
C7
Fm7
Fm7/C
yearn - ing,
while
16
Fm7/B♭
E♭
E♭/D
I'm
turn - ing a - round and a -
18
E♭/C
E♭/B
E♭/B♭
B♭7
E♭
round.
rit.

DON'T RAIN ON MY PARADE

(from "Funny Girl")

Words by
BOB MERRILL

Music by
JULE STYNE

CD/TRACK 1/20

14
A A+ A6 A A+ A6 B♭ B♭+ B♭6
Get read - y for me, love, 'cause I'm a "com - er." I sim - ply got - ta
17
B♭7 B♭6 B♭+ A/E A/F♯ A/E A/F♯
Allargando (in 4)
E/C♯ F♯/D♯
march, my heart's a drum - mer. No - bod - y, no, no - bod - y is gon - na
mf
21
E C
Tempo I
f
B B+ B6 F♯m7 E/G♯ B+/A B B+ B6 F♯m7 E/G♯ B+/A
rain on my pa - rade!
f
26
B B+ B6 F♯m7 E/G♯ B+/A B B+ B6 N.C. B
ff
sfz

EVEN THOUGH

(from "I Love You Because")

Lyrics by
RYAN CUNNINGHAM

Music by
JOSHUA SALZMAN

CD/TRACK 1/21

Medium pop ballad (♩ = 80)

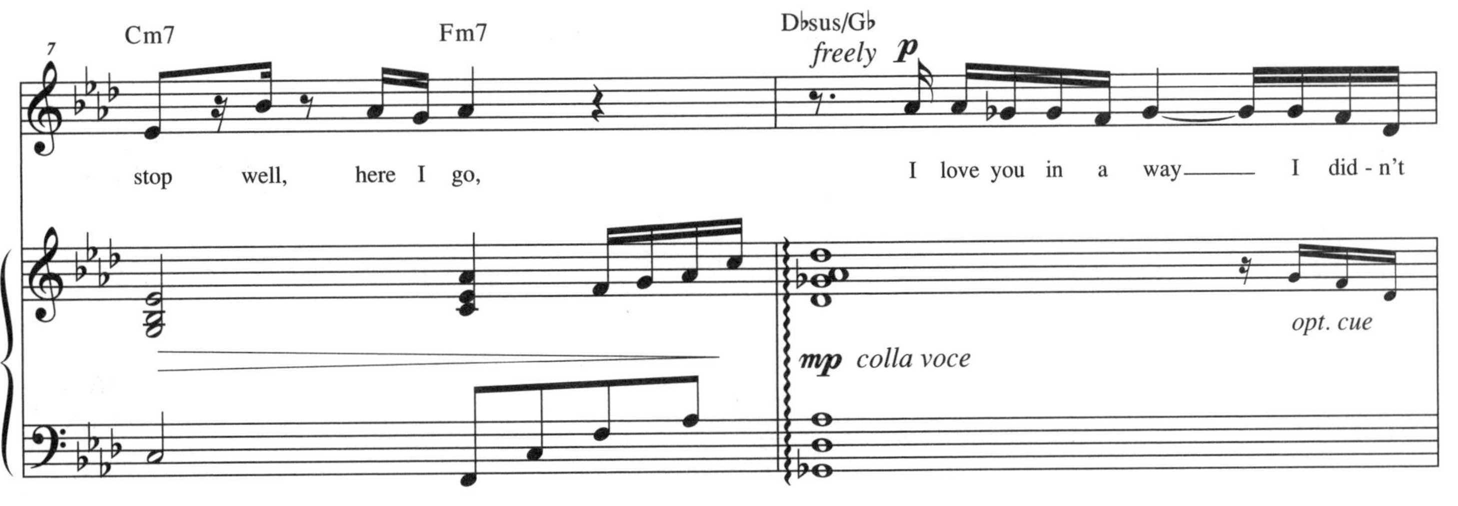
Cm7
Fm7
Db sus/Gb
freely
p
stop well, here I go,
I love you in a way I did-n't
mp colla voce
opt. cue

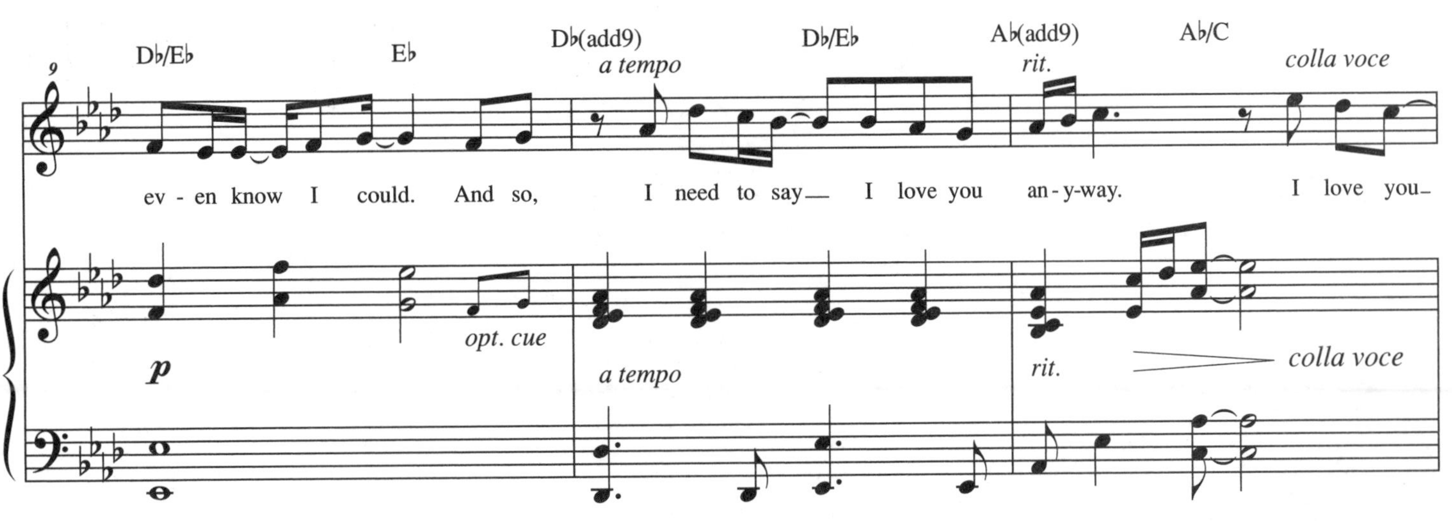
Db/Eb
Eb
Db(add9)
a tempo
Db/Eb
Ab(add9)
rit.
Ab/C
colla voce
ev-en know I could. And so, I need to say I love you an-y-way. I love you
opt. cue
p
a tempo
rit.
colla voce

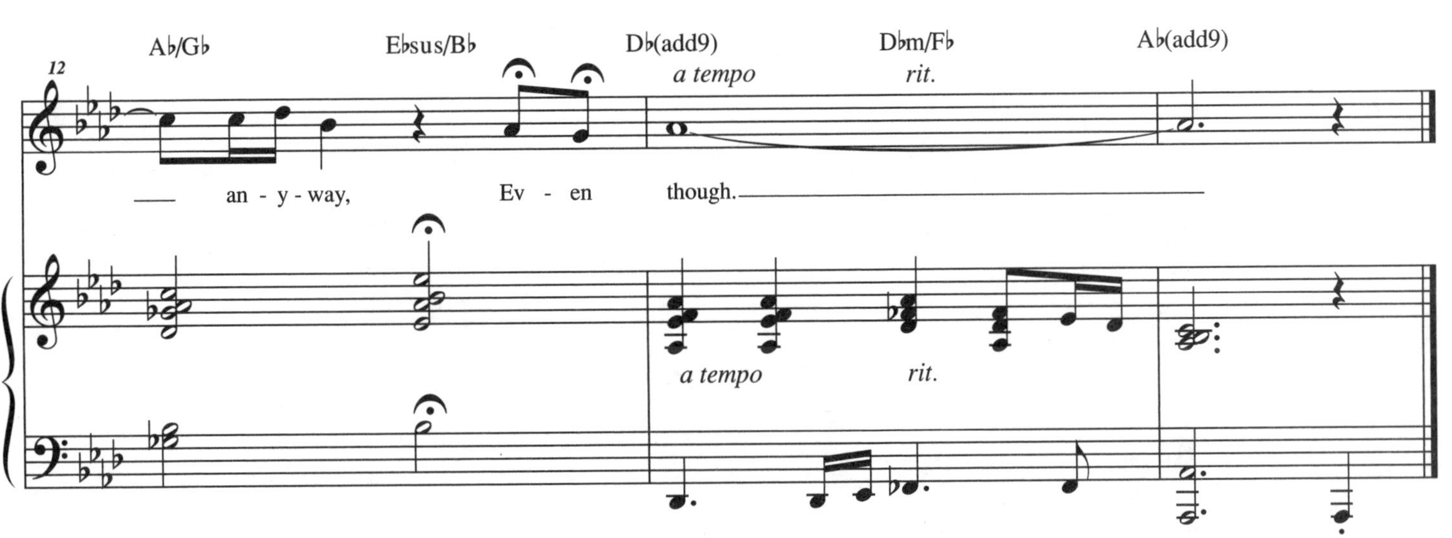
Ab/Gb
Ebsus/Bb
Db(add9)
a tempo
Dbm/Fb
rit.
Ab(add9)
an-y-way, Ev-en though.
a tempo
rit.

FUNNY

(from "My Favorite Year")

Lyrics by
LYNN AHRENS

Music by
STEPHEN FLAHERTY

CD/TRACK 1/22

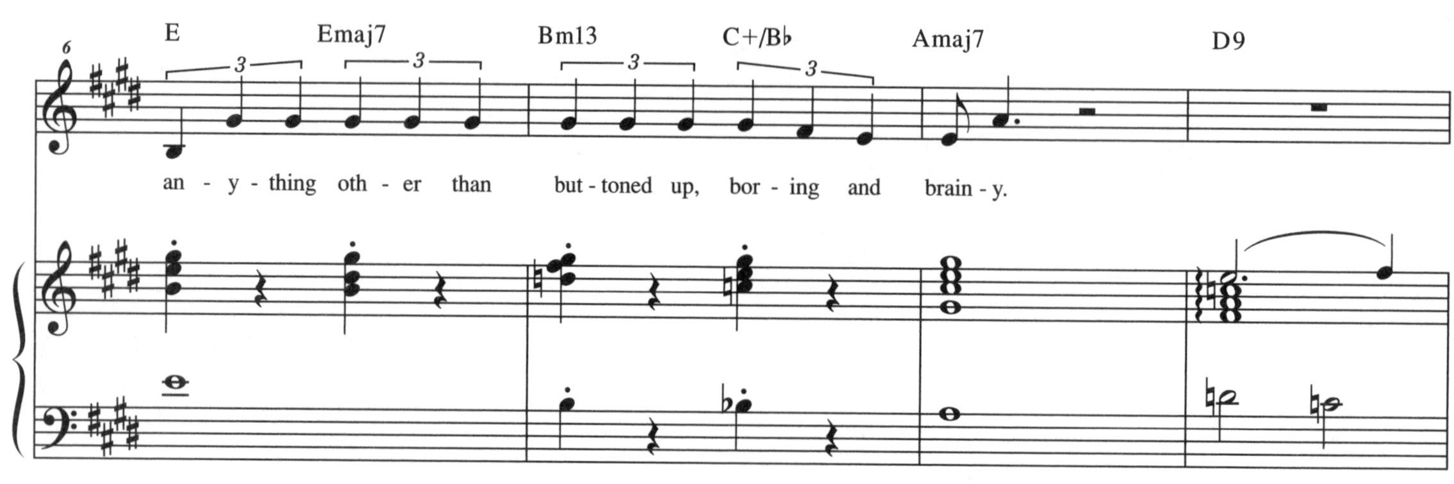

14
E/F♯
B7sus
B7
E(add9)
B♭7(♭5)
Amaj7
fun - ny like him. He's Grou - cho Marx and
19
A7
G♯m11
C♯m7
F♯m11
A/B
B7
Mick-ey Mouse and Fred As - taire, but I re - treat the more he plays the
(with pedal)
24
E
Bm7
B♭9(♭5)
Amaj7
A7
clown. Last week, he left a whoo-pee cush - ion
28
G♯m11
C♯7
F♯7sus
C♯m7
F♯7
F♯m7 B7sus
on my chair. Was I sup - posed to take that sit - ting down?

FUNNY HONEY

(from "Chicago")

Lyrics by
FRED EBB

Music by
JOHN KANDER

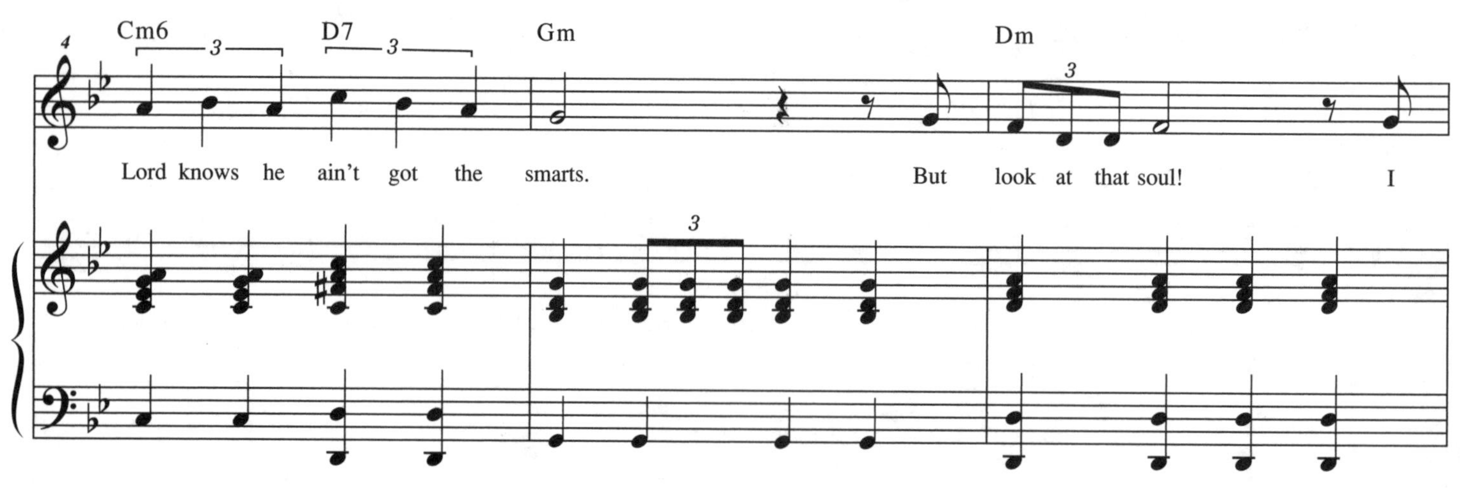

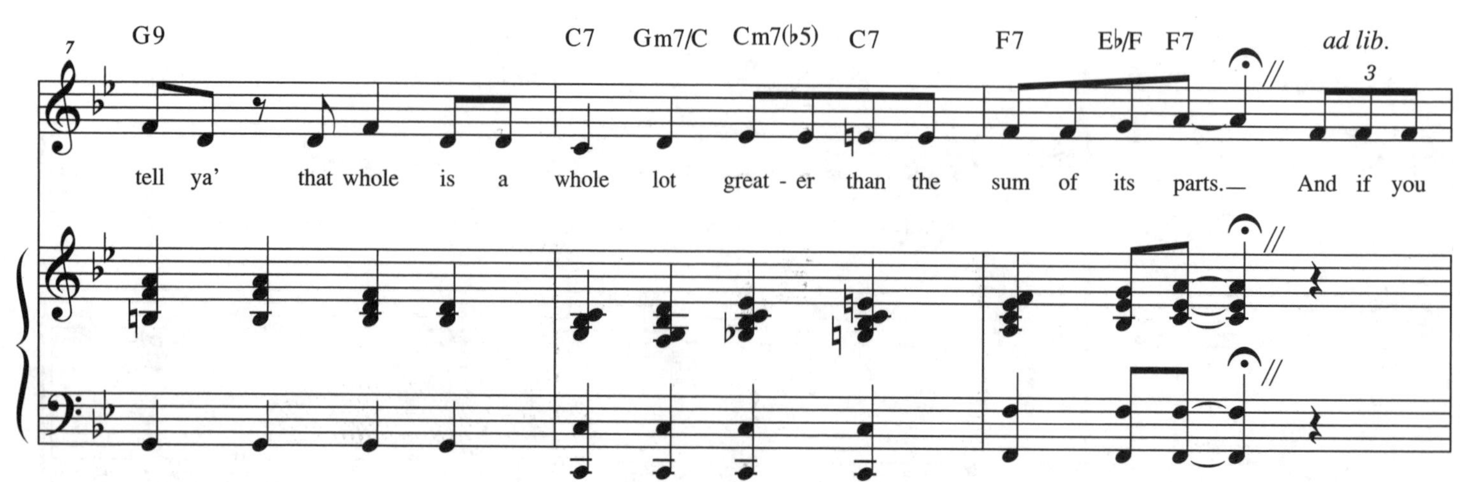

10
F7
F+7
a tempo
B♭
knew him like me, I know you'd a - gree. What if the world
mp a tempo
13
B♭+
B♭6
B♭9
slan - dered my name? Why he'd be right there tak - ing the blame.
16
E♭
E♭m6
Dm7
G7 F/A B♭dim7 G7/B
He loves me so and it all suits me fine, That
20
Cm7
Dm7
E♭
F9
B♭
B♭/F B9 B♭
sun - ny, fun - ny dum - my hub - by of mine.
ff

GET HAPPY

(from the film "Summer Stock")

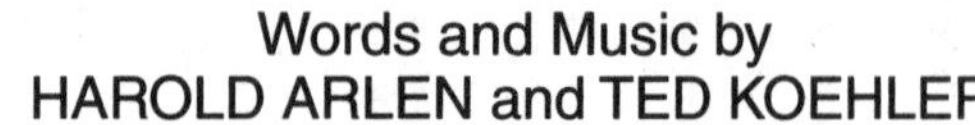

Words and Music by
HAROLD ARLEN and TED KOEHLER

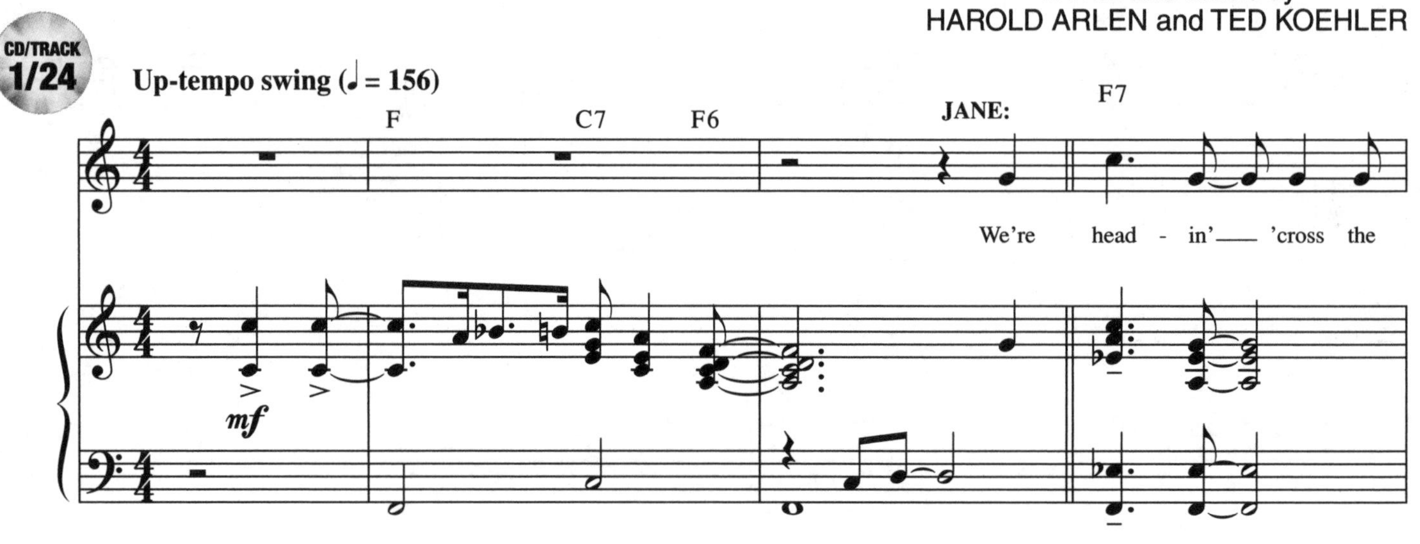

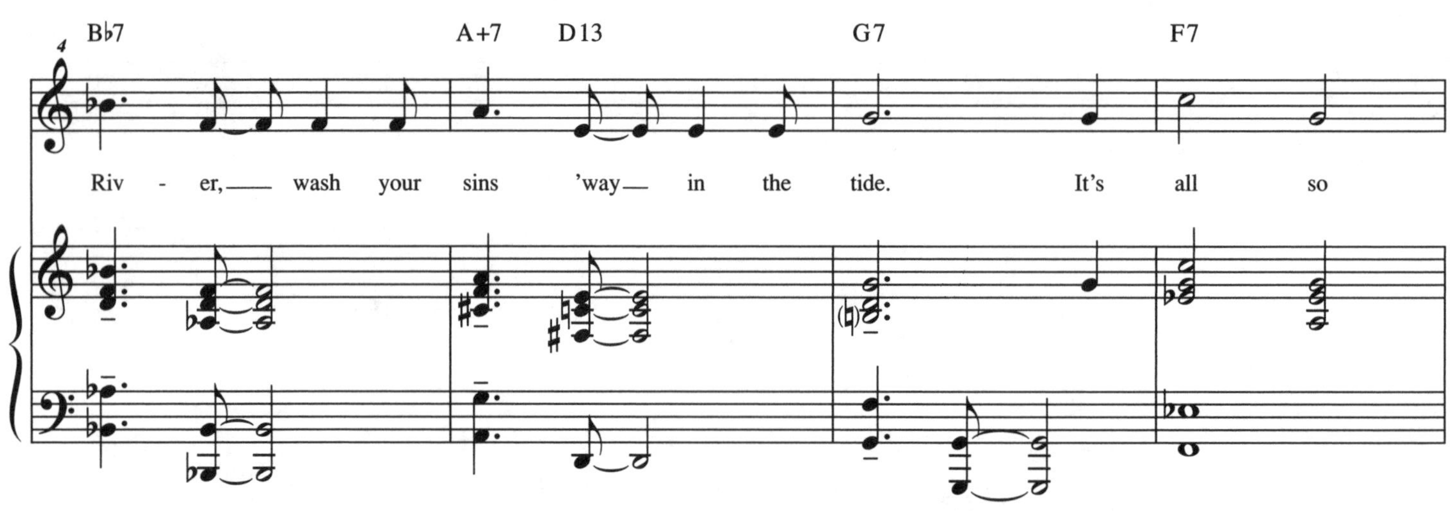

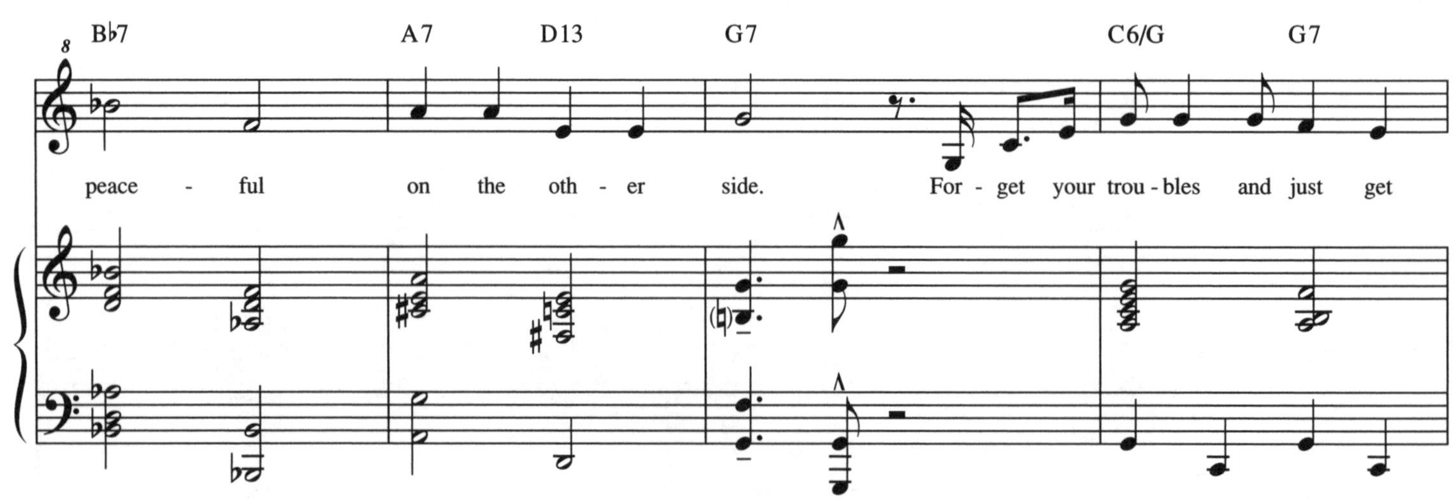

12
C6/G
G7
C6/G
G7
F/G
C/G
C6/G
G7
hap - py. You bet - ter chase all your cares a - way.
Shout "Hal - le - lu - jah!" Come on, get
16
C6/G
G7
C/G
G7
C
hap - py. Get read - y for the judge - ment day.

GIMME, GIMME

(from "Thoroughly Modern Millie")

Lyrics by
DICK SCANLAN

Music by
JEANINE TESORI

B♭m6
F/C
D7
G9
Sing, spar-row! Gim - me fat boy's fa - mous ar - row! Gim - me
C9
F6
F6/E♭
gim - me that thing called love!
Dm7(♭5)
D♭7
C9
F6
F6/E♭
Dm7(♭5)
D♭7
C9
F6
F6/E♭
Dm7(♭5)
D♭7
C9
E/C
F

GOOD MORNING
(from "Singin' in the Rain")

Words by
ARTHUR FREED

Music by
NACIO HERB BROWN

19
C G7/D C/E G7/D C G7/D C/E
When we left the movie show, the future wasn't bright. But
23
E♭/G Fm7 B♭7 E♭/G Fm7(♭5) B♭ A♭/B♭ Gm/B♭ B♭9 E♭7 Cm E♭7/B♭
came the dawn. The show goes on! I don't want to say good night. So say good
27
A♭ E♭7 A♭ B dim7
morn - ing, good morn - ing. Rain - bows are shin - ing through. Good
31
E♭7/B♭ E♭7 A♭ B♭m/E♭ Cm/E♭ A♭6
morn - ing, good morn - ing to you!

GOOD MORNING STARSHINE

(from "Hair")

Words by
JAMES RADO and
GEROME RAGNI

Music by
GALT MACDERMOT

Bb C Bb A7(b9) Dm F7 Bb Ab7(#11) G7 C7
long, my love and me as we sing our early morning sing-
F Optional ending F Gm7 C7
ing song. Glid-dy glup gloo-py nib-by nab-by noo-py la la la lo lo.
Gm7 C7 Gm C7 Gm7 C7 F6
Sab-ba sib-by sab-ba noo-by ab-ba nab-ba le le lo lo.
Bb A7 Dm Gm F/C Gm C7sus F
Too-by oo-by wal-la noo-by ab-ba nab-ba, Ear-ly morn-ing sing-ing song.
p
8va

HANGIN' AROUND WITH YOU

(from "Strike Up the Band"–1930)

Music and Lyrics by
GEORGE GERSHWIN and IRA GERSHWIN

15 G13 G13(♭9) G7 C9 C7(♭9)
see that I'm like - ly to be
18 C7(♭5) C7 C+7 F F7/C B♭ Gm7 F F7/C B♭ Gm7
on the shelf. If you want me hang-in' a-round with you, hang-in' a-round with
21 F B♭ Gm7 F F/A A♭dim7 C7/G G♯dim7
you, hang-in' a-round with you, dear - ie, you've got to learn, you've
24 D9/A Fdim/A♭ C7/G C7 N.C. F
got to learn to be your - self.
mp
f

HERE'S WHERE I STAND

(from the film "Camp")

Words by
LYNN AHRENS

Music by
MICHAEL GORE

F
C/E
Dm
F/C
B♭
F/A
10
stand.
Here's
who
I
am.
Love
me,
love
me,
Gm7
B♭/F
B♭/C
13
love
me
and
we'll
make
it
through.
I'm
B♭
F/A
Gm7
Gm7
F/A
G7/B
B♭/C
16
freely
count - ing,
I'm
count - ing,
I'm
count - ing,
I'm
count-ing
on
freely
20
B♭
F/A
Gm7
F
you.
slowly
sfz

HOLD ON
(from "The Secret Garden")

Lyrics by
MARSHA NORMAN

Music by
LUCY SIMON

C♯m
G♯m
A
F♯7sus
F♯
do then is you tell your - self to wait it out. You say, "It's this
E
A/C♯
E(add9)/B
A
A/B
C♯m
Bsus
day, not me, that's bound to go a - way," Child- Hold
E/F♯
F♯7
E
A/C♯
E(add9)/B
A/F♯
Amaj7/G♯
F♯m/A
A/B
on. It's this day not you that's bound to go a -
Esus
E
D6/E
rall.
E(add9)
E
way.
rall.
(with pedal)

HOME
(from "The Wiz")

Words and Music by
CHARLIE SMALLS

CD/TRACK 1/31

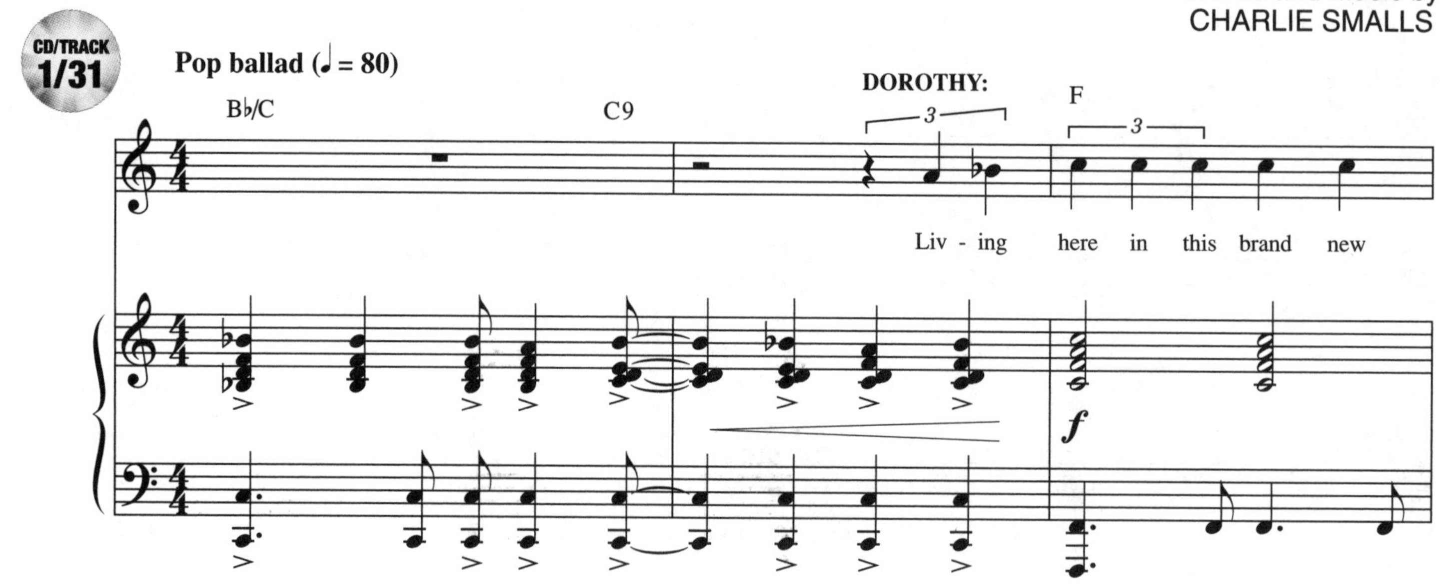

10
C9
B♭/D
C7/E
F
G/F
3
And I've learned that we must look in - side our hearts to
13
Em7
A7(♭9)
Dm7
find a world full of love like yours, like
17
A♭/B♭
B♭9
C
mine, like home.
20
E♭/D♭
C
fff

HOW ARE THINGS IN GLOCCA MORRA?

(from "Finian's Rainbow")

Words by
E.Y. HARBURG

Music by
BURTON LANE

Gb/Bb Fm/Ab G/Ab Ab7(b9) Ab7/Db Db Ab7/Db Db F+7
dream - y there not to see me there? So I
Gb Ab7/Gb Ebm Db/F F+7 Gb Ab7/Gb Ebm Db/F F+7
ask each weep - ing wil - low, and each brook a - long the way, and each
Gb Fm Ab6 Db(add9) Ddim7
lad that comes a whist - lin' "Too - ra - lay." How are
Ebm Fm Gbmaj7/Ab Ab7 Db6/9 Db
rit.
things in Gloc - ca Mor - ra this fine day?

HOW COULD I EVER KNOW?

(from "The Secret Garden")

Lyrics by
MARSHA NORMAN

Music by
LUCY SIMON

CD/TRACK 1/33

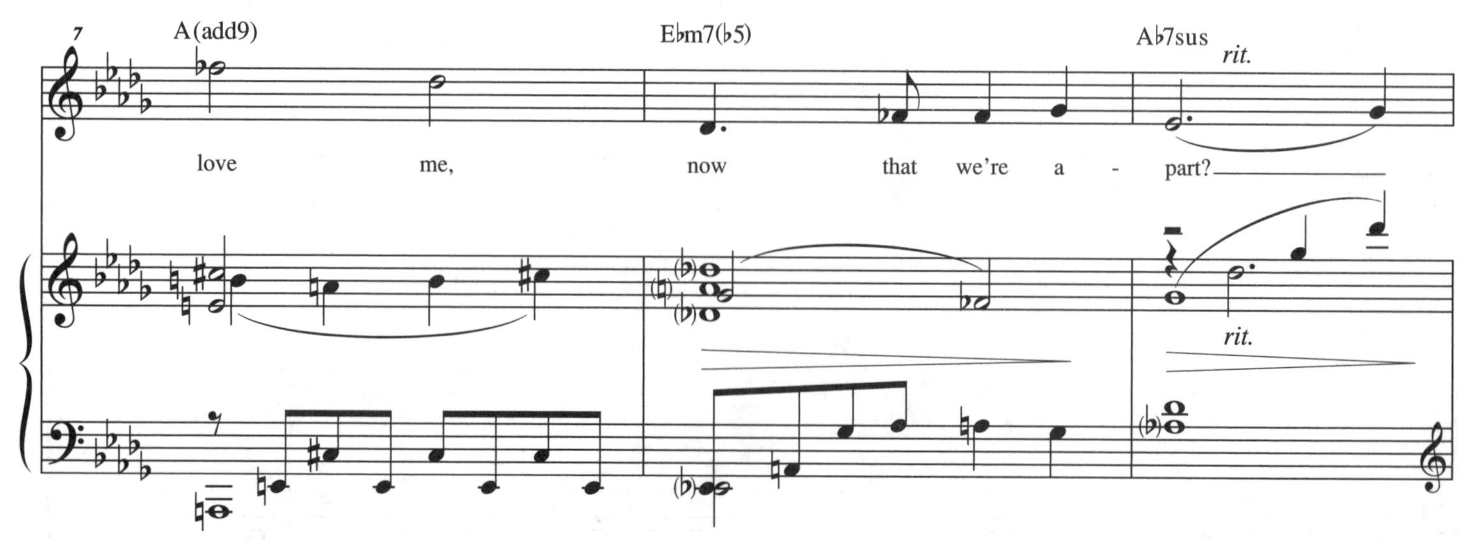

meno mosso
Db(add9)
pp
How could I know I would nev - er hold you?
Ab7sus/Db
Never a - gain in this
world, but oh,
più passionato
Ebm7
cresc.
sure as you breathe, I am there in - side you.
Db/F
B7/A
Db/Ab
Fm7
Gb(add9)
Gb/Ab
Bbm7
rit.
Bbm7/Ab
How could I ev - er know?
Gb(add9)
Gb/Ab
Db(add9)
a tempo
Gb/Db
molto rit.
Db
How could I ev - er know?

I CAN COOK, TOO

(from "On the Town")

Lyrics by
BETTY COMDEN and
ADOLPH GREEN

Music by
LEONARD BERNSTEIN

11
F♯7
B7
man's i - deal of a per - fect meal, right down to the dem - i - tasse.
I'm a
15
E9
A7
Am/D
D9
pot of joy for a hun - gry boy, Ba - by, I'm cook - ing with gas! Oh, I'm a
19
G6
C9
G6
gum - drop, a sweet lol - li - pop, a brook trout right out of the
22
D/E
Dm/B♭
E7
A9
Am7
D7(♭9)
G
D♭dim7
C7
G6/9
brook, and what's more ba - by, I can cook!

I COULD HAVE DANCED ALL NIGHT

(from "My Fair Lady")

Lyrics by
ALAN JAY LERNER

Music by
FREDERICK LOEWE

CD/TRACK 1/35

11 Dm
Dm(maj7)
Dm7
spread my wings and done a thou - sand
14 Dm6
F/G
G7
F/G
G+7
Cmaj9
C6
things I've nev - er done be - fore.
Optional start
18
Cmaj7 C N.C.
E(add9)
F♯m7/B
B7
I'll nev - er know what made it so ex -
21 E
Emaj7
E6
E N.C.
G(add9)
Am/D
D7(♭9)
- cit - ing, why all at once my heart took

25 G9
F Cmaj7 Dm7 C(add9)
f ten. ten. ten. a tempo
Cmaj9
flight. I on - ly know, when
ten. ten. ten.
f
ten. ten. ten.
a tempo
28
F6 F Dm7
he be - gan to dance with me, I could have
31 Dm7/G
G7
f
danced, danced, danced all
f
34 Cmaj7
D/C D♭/G C
night.
ff

I GET A KICK OUT OF YOU

(from "Anything Goes")

Words and Music by
COLE PORTER

G7
Dm7
G7
C
Em
me.
I get no kick in a plane,
Dm7
cresc.
G7
Em7
Am7
Dm7
dim.
fly - ing too high with some guy in the sky is my i - dea of
G7
B♭9(♯11)
A9
Dm7
ad lib.
G9
noth - ing to do.
Yet I get a kick out of
mp
C6
a tempo
you.

I GOT RHYTHM
(from "Girl Crazy")

Music and Lyrics by
GEORGE GERSHWIN and IRA GERSHWIN

17 B♭ B♭6 Cm7 F7 B♭/F F7 B♭ E♭9/B♭
I got my man; who could ask for an - y - thing more?
Optional start
21 D7 C/D Dm7(♭5) D9 G D+ G11 G7
Old Man Trou - ble, I don't mind him.
25 C7 C11 Cm7(♭5) C9 G♭7(♭5) F7
You won't find him 'round my door!
29 B♭ B♭6 Cm7 F7 Dm7 D♭dim7 Cm7 F7
I got star - light, I got sweet dreams,

Bb
Bb6
Cm7
F7
Bb
Ab6
G7
f
I got my man; who could ask for an-y-thing more? Who could
C9
F7
Bb
ff
Bb6
Cm7
F7
Bb/F
F9
F7
Bb
ask for an-y-thing more?
8va
sfz

I HAD MYSELF A TRUE LOVE

(from "St. Louis Woman")

Words by
JOHNNY MERCER

Music by
HAROLD ARLEN

CD/TRACK 1/38

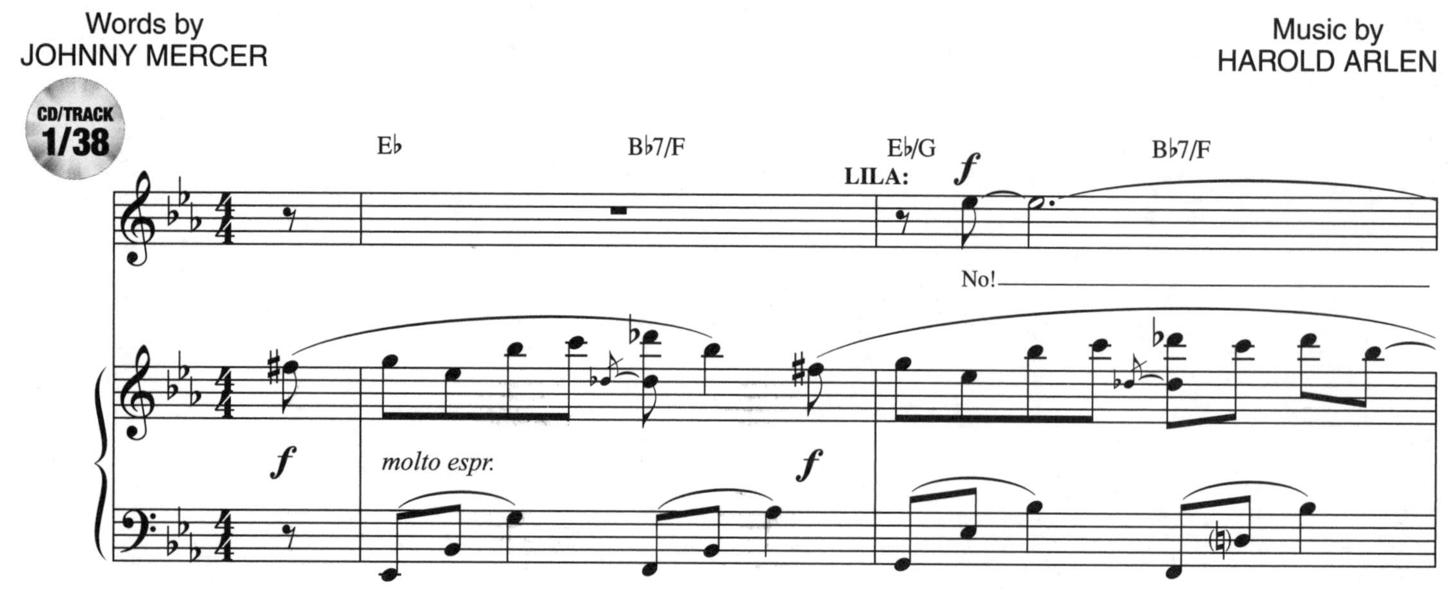

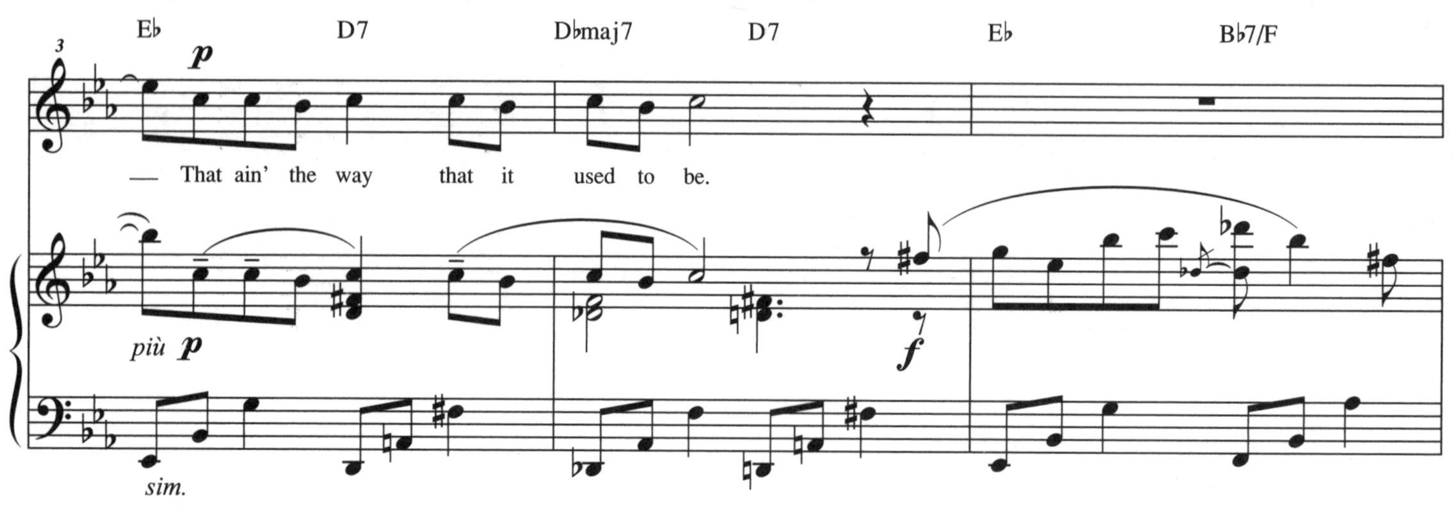

A♭maj7
F7/A
A♭m6
E♭/G
G♭dim7
may be a lot of things I miss, a lot of things I don't know, but I
F+7
Gm7(♭5)
C7
Fm7
E♭/G
F+7(♭9)
B♭7
rit.
do know this: Now I ain' got no love an' once up - on a time I had a
(cues)
rit.
a tempo
E♭
B♭7/A♭
Gm(maj7)
Gm7(♭5)
true love.
p a tempo molto espr.
C7/G
C♭/G♭
E♭
rit.
R.H.
pp
R.H.
L.H.

I LOVED YOU ONCE IN SILENCE

(from "Camelot")

Lyrics by
ALAN JAY LERNER

Music by
FREDERICK LOEWE

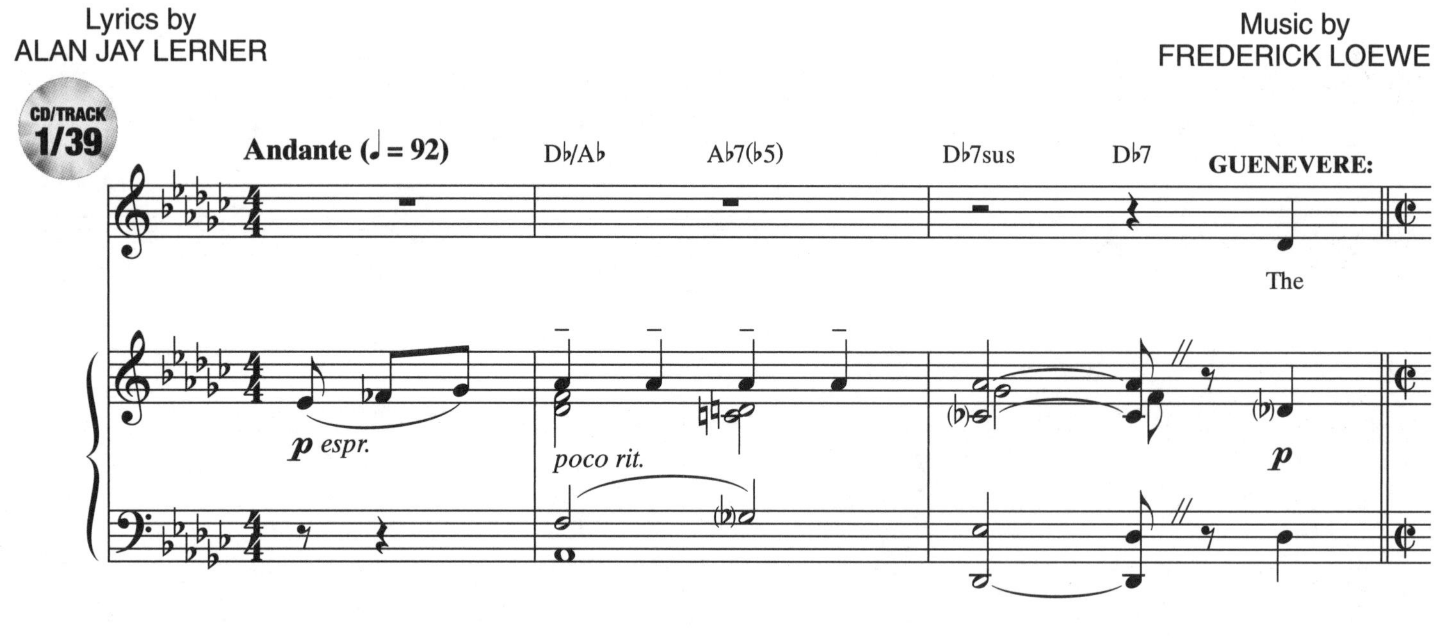

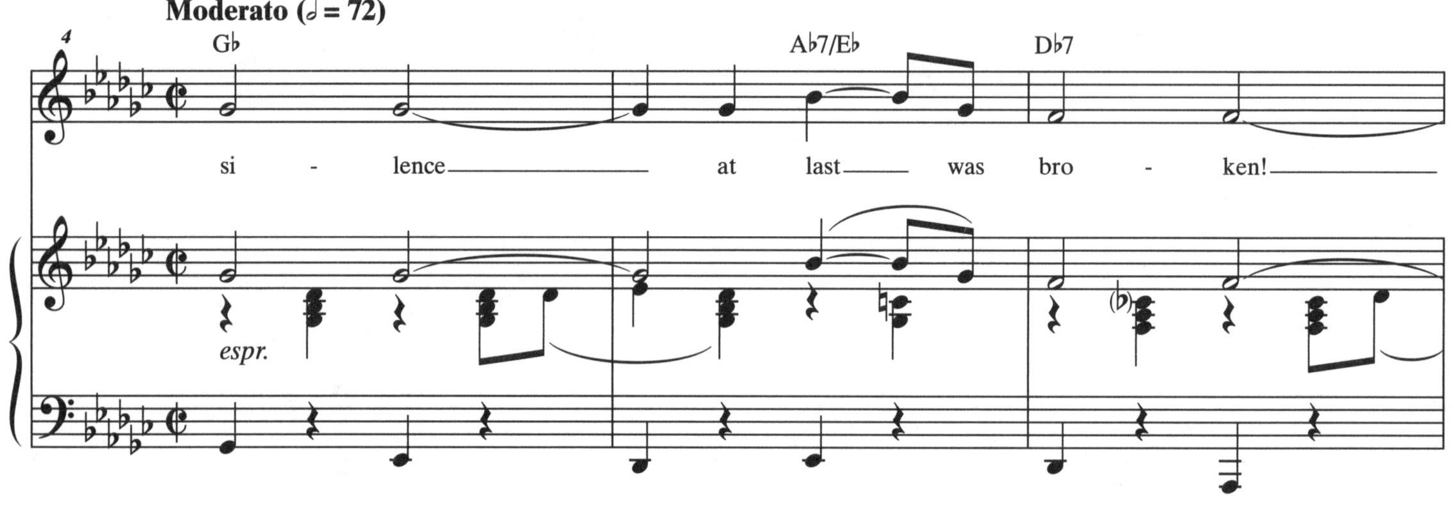

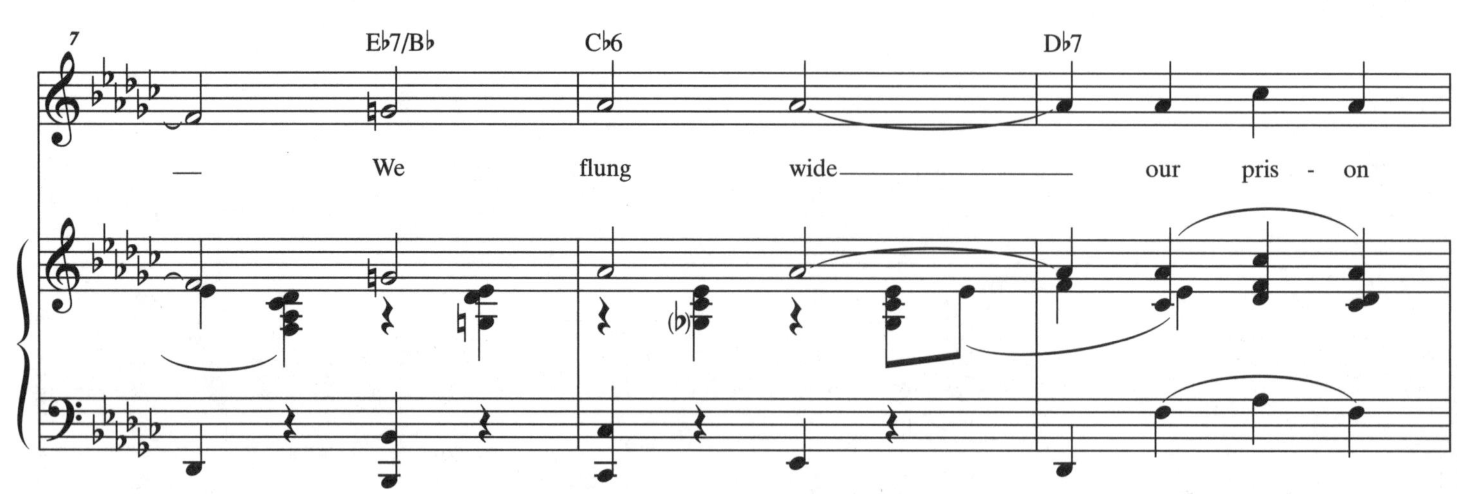

I Loved You Once in Silence - 2 - 1
34277

10
Gb Gb6 Gb Gb/Bb Db7/Ab
door. Ev - 'ry joy - ous
13
Gb7 Cb Ab7(b5)/C Cb/Db D7
poco rit. rall.
word of love was spo - ken... And now there's
poco rit. rall.
sfz
Andante (♩ = 100)
16
Gb/Db Db7 Bbm Ebm Db/F Gb6 Gb7 Cb Ebm7 Gdim7 Abm7
colla voce
twice as much grief, twice the strain for us, twice the de - spair, twice the pain for us
colla voce
19
Gb/Db Gb7/Db Cb Db7 Cb/Gb Gb
poco rubato
as we had known be - fore.
poco rubato

I SPEAK SIX LANGUAGES

(from "The 25th Annual Putnam County Spelling Bee")

Words and Music by
WILLIAM FINN

10
A7
C
B7(♯9)
un - a - mazed am I. Win - ning is a job from which I get
13
Em7
A7
A♭+7
G
no real en - joy - ment, but...
I
16
D/F♯
Fm6
C/E
speak six lan - gua - ges.
That's
19
E♭6
G
one, two, three, four, five,...
six.
8va

I THINK I MAY WANT TO REMEMBER TODAY

(from "Starting Here, Starting Now")

Words by
RICHARD MALTBY, JR.

Music by
DAVID SHIRE

23
D♭maj9
Dm7(♭5)
f
A♭/E♭
A♭+/E♭
Al - bert, Al - bert, I think I may want to re -
29
D♭/E♭
Cm/E♭
D♭/E♭
mem - ber, Re - mem - ber this tenth of Oc - to - ber. I
35
Cm/E♭
cresc.
Fm/E♭
D♭maj7/E♭
D♭/E♭
ff
A♭maj13
know I shall want to re - mem - ber to - day!
42
E♭7sus/B♭
A♭maj9/C
D♭maj7
Fm7/E♭
A♭maj9

I WANT IT NOW

(from "Willy Wonka And The Chocolate Factory")

Words and Music by
LESLIE BRICUSSE and ANTHONY NEWLEY

Demanding
29
Ab6
Ab/Bb
Bb7
Ab/Bb
Bb+
Eb6
Eb6/Bb
Eb6
F/Eb
I want the works!
I want the whole works.
mf
36
Eb
Ebmaj7
F/Eb
Fm7
F7
Gm7
Abmaj7
Pres - ents and priz - es and sweets and sur - pris - es of all shapes and siz - es and now.
43
Am7(b5)
Eb/Bb
Bb9
Bb7sus
Bb7
Eb6
Don't care how, I want it now.
49
Bb
Bbsus
Bb(b5)
Bb(no3rd)
Bb+
Bb6
Bb7(#5)
Eb
Don't care how, I want it now!

I WANT TO GO TO HOLLYWOOD

(from "Grand Hotel")

Words and Music by
MAURY YESTON

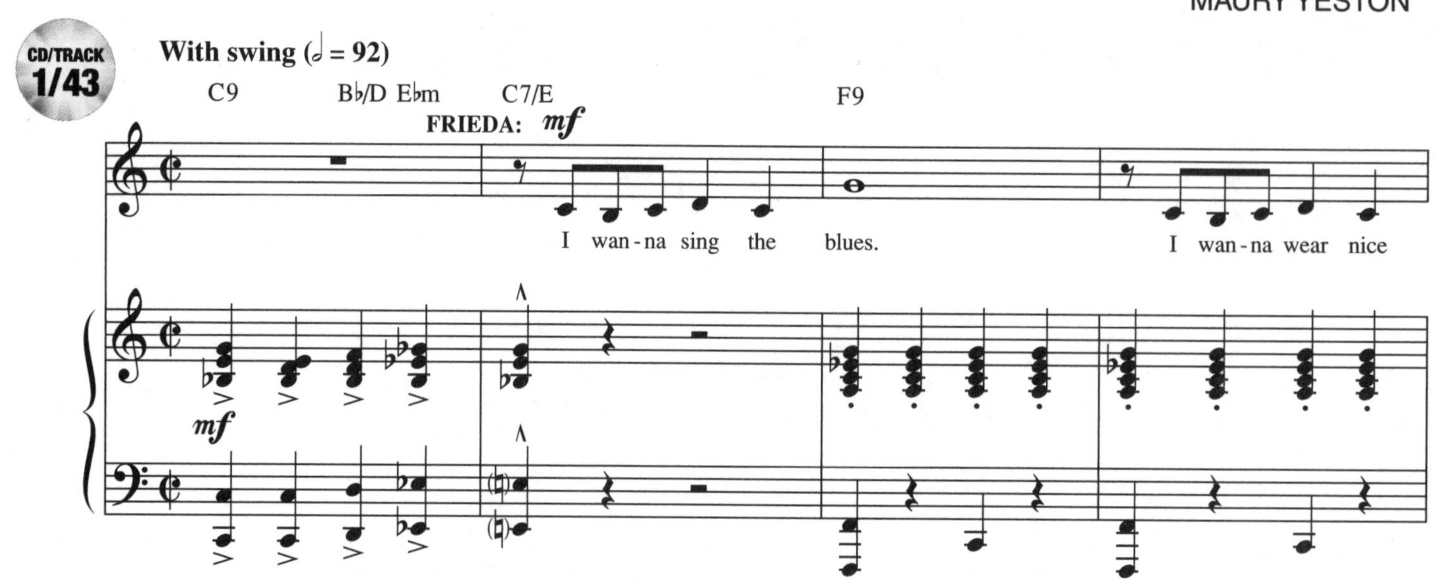

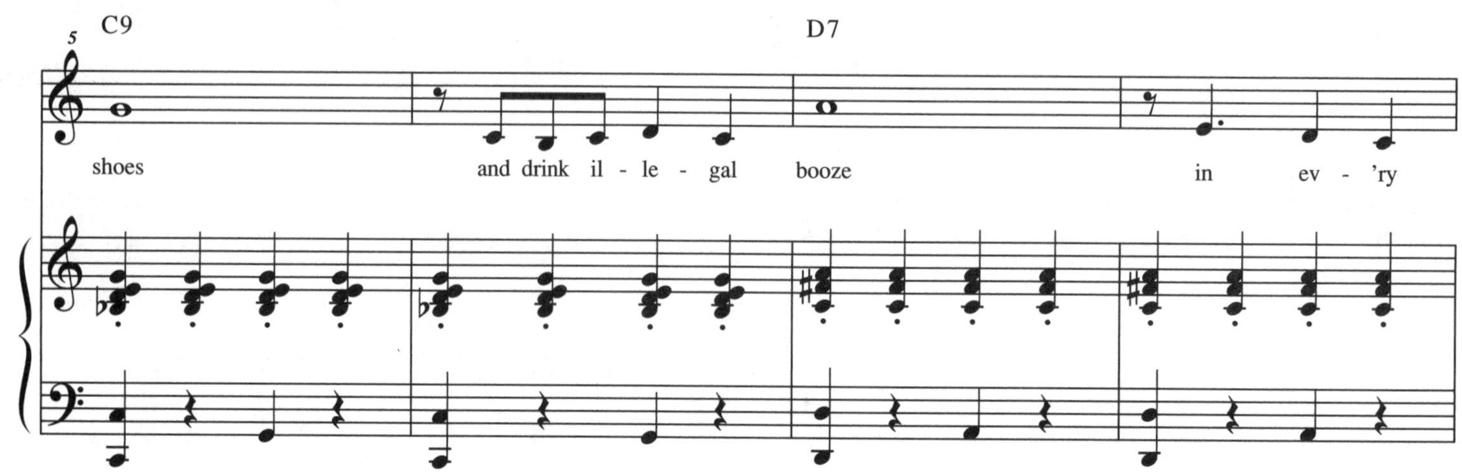

13
C G+ Gm/C G+ C G+ Gm/C G+
If I'm a big box of - fice win - ner there, I'll be the most well known Ber - lin - er there
17
A7(♭9) G/B A7/C♯ A7 G/B A7/C♯ D7(add4) G7sus G7
ev - er was! I want to go to Hol - ly...
21
D7 F/G G9 F/G G7(♯9) G7
I have to go, I have to go to Hol - ly -
25
C G+ Gm/C G+ C G+ Gm/C G+ C
- wood!

I WISH I WERE IN LOVE AGAIN

(from "Babes in Arms")

Words by
LORENZ HART

Music by
RICHARD RODGERS

CD/TRACK 1/44

10
Cmaj7 Cm6 G/B E7 A7 D7 G G7
No more pain! No more strain!
14
Cmaj7 Cm6 G/B E7(♭9) A7
Now I'm sane, but I would rath - er be
17
D7 Gmaj7 Gdim7 Gmaj7
ga - ga! Be - lieve me sir, I much pre - fer the clas - sic bat - tle of a
21
Gdim7 Gmaj7 B7 Em Am7 D7 G
him and her. I don't like qui - et and I wish I were in love a - gain!
8va

I'M A STRANGER HERE MYSELF

(from "One Touch Of Venus")

Lyrics by
OGDEN NASH

Music by
KURT WEILL

9
Em7(♭5)
rit.
Am7(♭5)
a tempo
D7
Gm6
E♭7(♯11)
ask, And no one un - der - stands.
Love me, or leave me, that
rit.
a tempo
12
Gm6
E♭7(♯11)
Gm6
3
Cm7
3
D7(♭9)
seems to be the ques - tion; I don't know the tac - tics to use.
But
3
3
15
Am7(♭5)
E♭7(♯11)
A♭7(♭5)
D♭7(♭5)
Gm/D
E♭7
if he should of - fer a per - son - al sug - ges - tion, How could I pos - si - bly re -
18
Em7(♭5)
A7(♭9)
D7
Gm
- fuse, when I'm a stran - ger here my - self?
sf

I'M HERE

(from "The Color Purple")

Words and Music by QUINCY JONES,
ROD TEMPERTON, JEREMY LUBBOCK
and CHRISTOPHER BOARDMAN

CD/TRACK 1/46

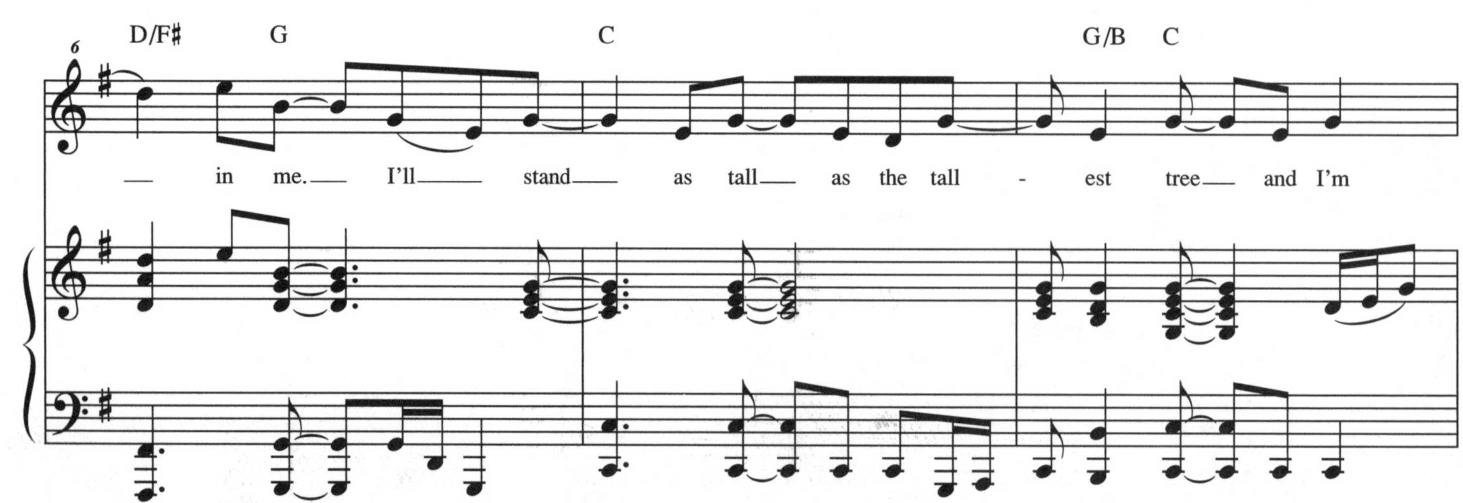

9
Am11
Bm11
thank-ful for — ev - 'ry day — that I'm giv - en,
both the eas - y and hard-
12
f
C6/9
mp freely
Dsus D Dsus
— ones I'm liv - in'. —
But most of all — I'm thank-ful for lov-ing who I
f
mp freely
15
Am11
D7sus
G6/9
real - ly am. — I'm beau-ti-ful, yes, I'm beau-ti-ful, — and I'm
18
G
here. —
mf

I'M NOT AT ALL IN LOVE

(from "The Pajama Game")

Words and Music by
RICHARD ADLER and JERRY ROSS

21
D/F♯
rall.
Bm7
Em7
A7
D
rall.
or if he has the rest of you sigh - in'. You may be
rall.
rall.
26
D7
G6
G
Em7(♭5)
D7/A
a tempo
Adim7
sold but this girl ain't buy - in'. I'm not at
a tempo
31
Em7/A
A13
D
E♭9(♯11)
all in love!
f
36
D
fff

IF YOU HADN'T, BUT YOU DID

(from "Two on the Aisle")

Lyrics by
BETTY COMDEN and
ADOLPH GREEN

Music by
JULE STYNE

CD/TRACK 1/48

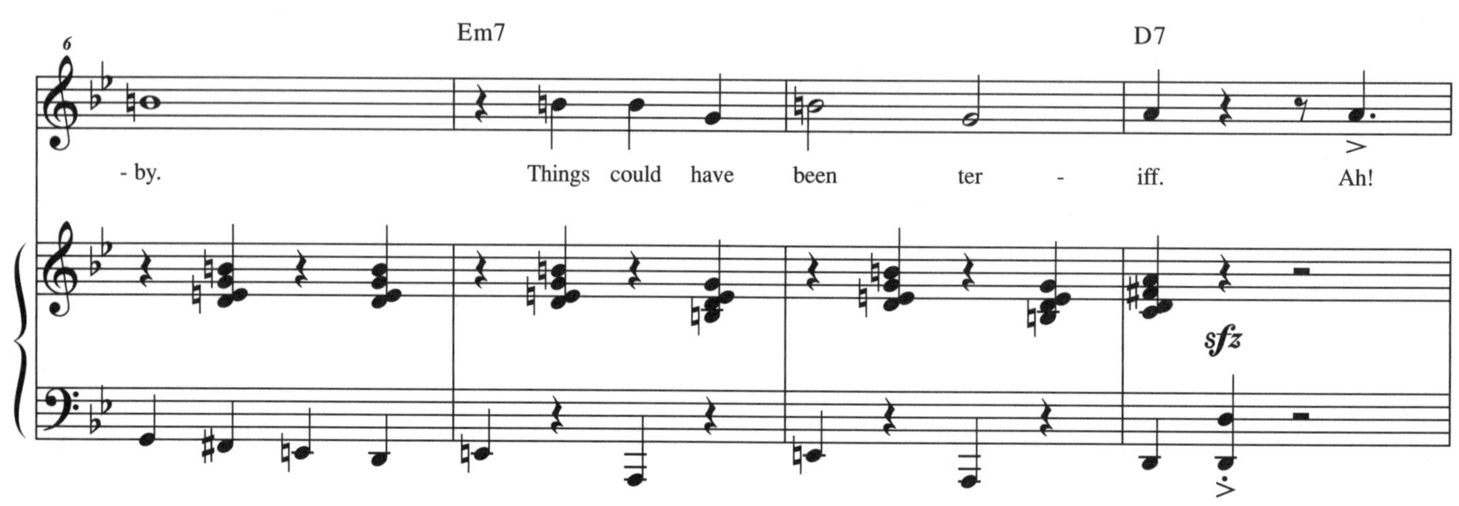

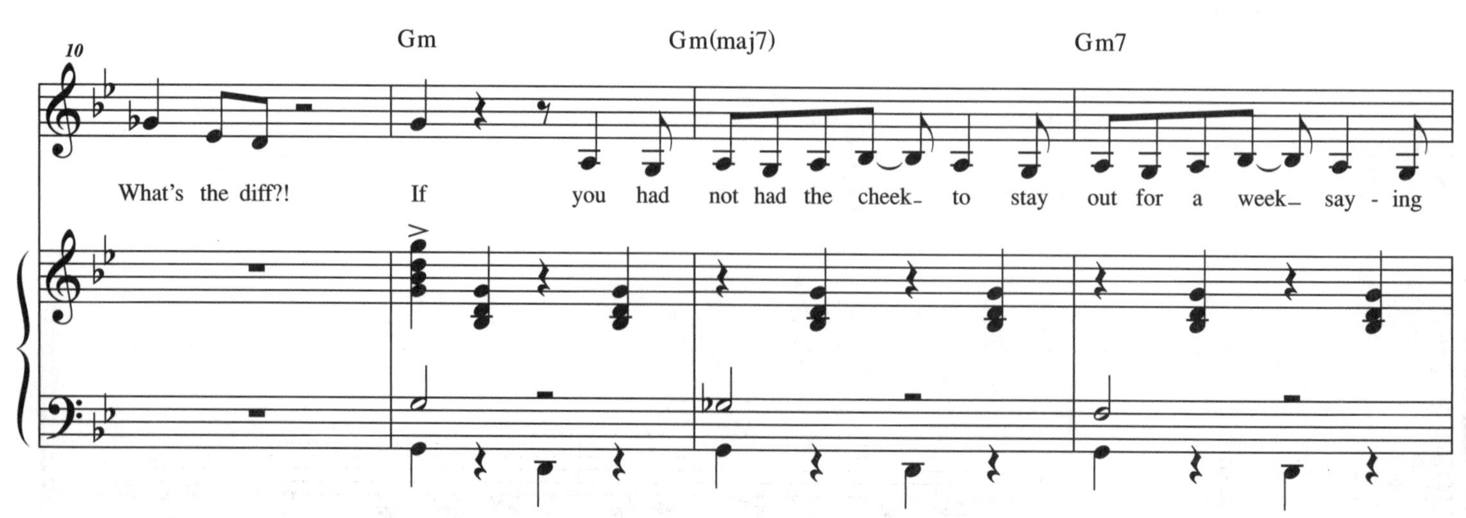

14
Gm6
Gm
Gm(maj7)
G7sus
"Back in a jiff!"
If you were not such a two - tim - ing guy.
18
G7
C6
C♯dim7
G6/D
Am7/D
If you were-n't, if you had-n't, if you did-n't, if you were-n't if you
22
B♭dim7/D
G6/D
Am7
B♭dim7
G/B
Em
C7/A
had-n't, if you did-n't. But you were and you have and you went and you did and so
26
D13(♭9)
Gm6
good - bye!

IS IT REALLY ME?

(from "110 in the Shade")

Words by
TOM JONES

Music by
HARVEY SCHMIDT

CD/TRACK 1/49

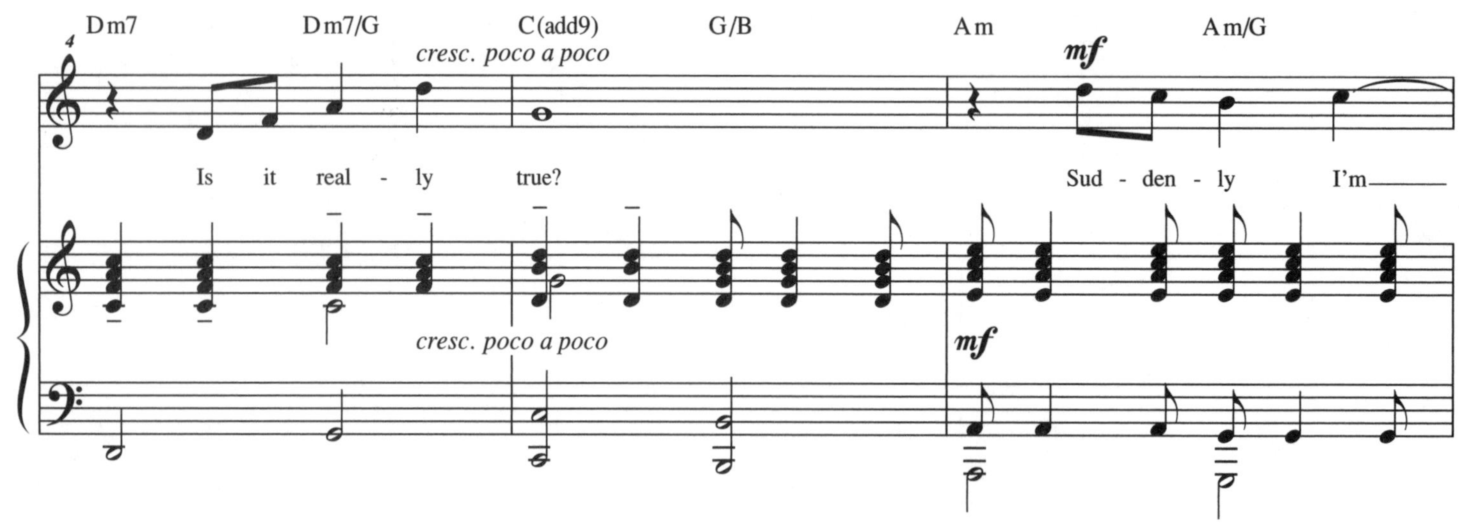

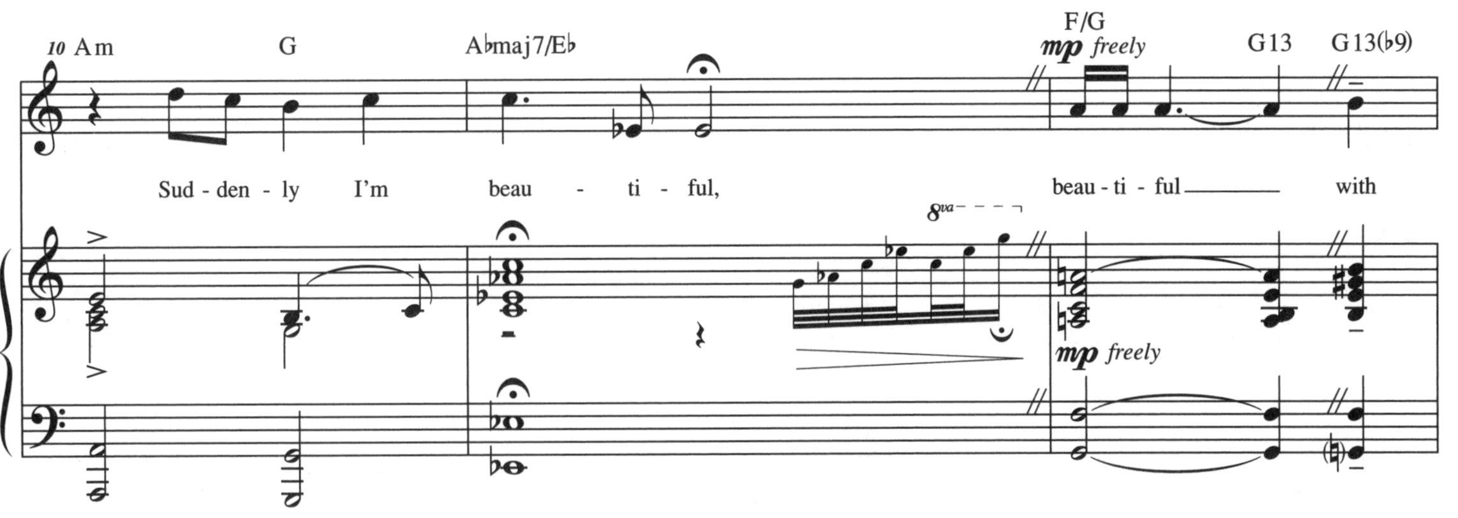
10 Am
G
A♭maj7/E♭
F/G
mp freely
G13
G13(♭9)
Sud - den - ly I'm beau - ti - ful,
beau - ti - ful
with
8va
mp freely

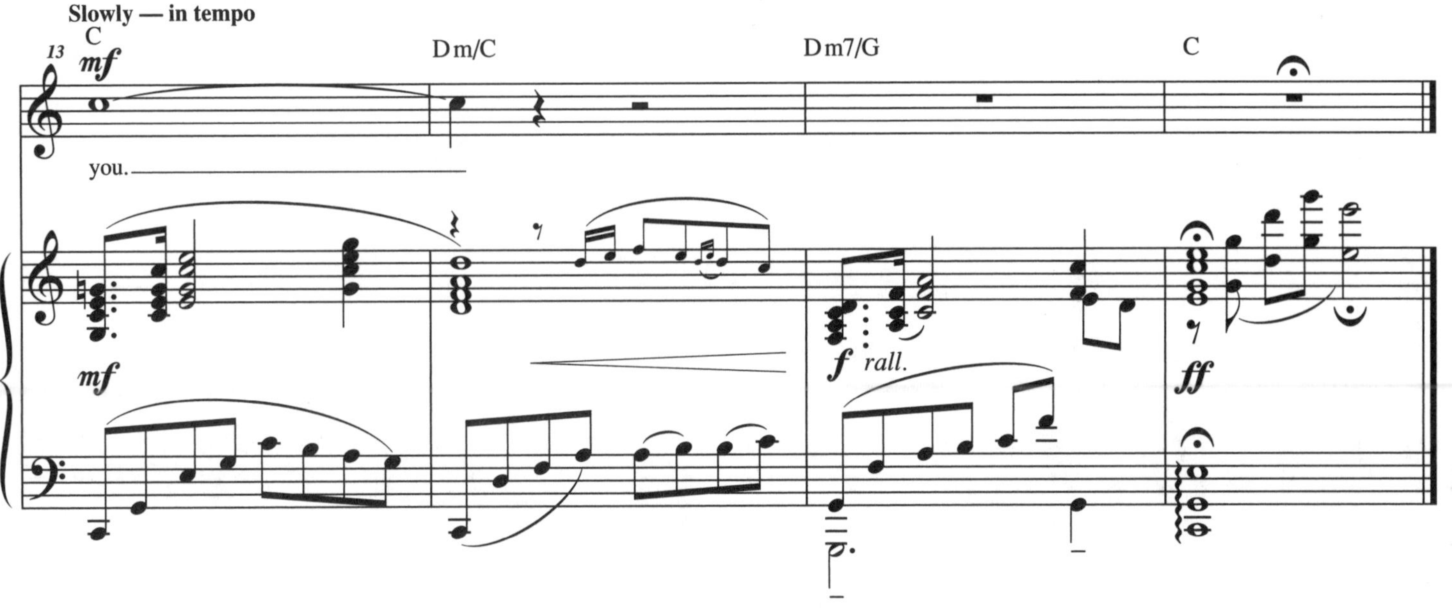
Slowly — in tempo
13 C
mf
Dm/C
Dm7/G
C
you.
mf
f rall.
ff

IT'S A PERFECT RELATIONSHIP

(from "Bells Are Ringing")

Words by BETTY COMDEN
and ADOLPH GREEN

Music by
JULE STYNE

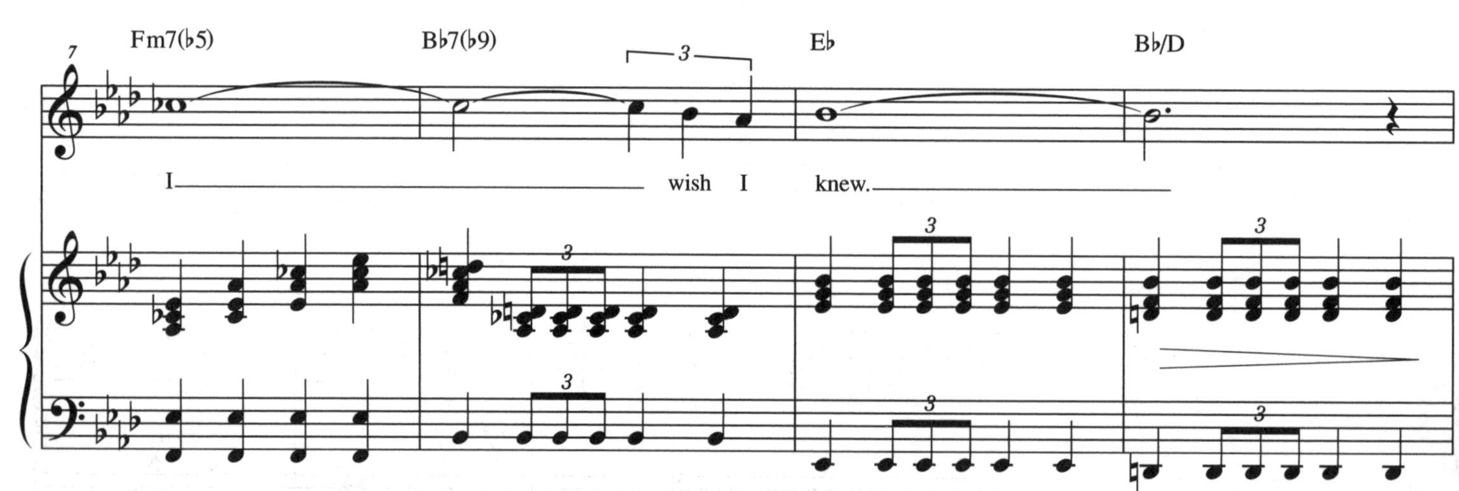

Db♭m7 G♭9 C♭ Fm7(♭5) E♭ B♭m7
p pp
What does he look like? Is he six-foot-sev-en or
three-foot-two? Has he eyes of brown or ba-by blue? Big and might-y or un-der-fed?
Trim black mus-tache or beard of red? Can he dance like Fred As-taire? Is he dark or
is he fair? Pom-pa-dour or not a hair? Well, I don't care!
E♭ D♭m6/F♭ B♭7 E♭7
mp
mf

LET'S PLAY A LOVE SCENE

(from "Fame: The Musical")

Lyrics by
JACQUES LEVY

Music by
STEVE MARGOSHES

CD/TRACK 2/1

D♯sus
D♯
G♯m
F♯sus
F♯
A/B
B
Find a way— to start— and play it from— the heart,— a per - fect
E
D♯
G♯m
G7
B/F♯
E♯m7(♭5)
scene from a play— un - known. Let's play a love scene,
E/F♯
freely
love— scene of our
B
B7/A
E/G♯
G7
B
a tempo
own.
p a tempo

LIGHT
(from "Next to Normal")

Lyrics by
BRIAN YORKEY

Music by
TOM KITT

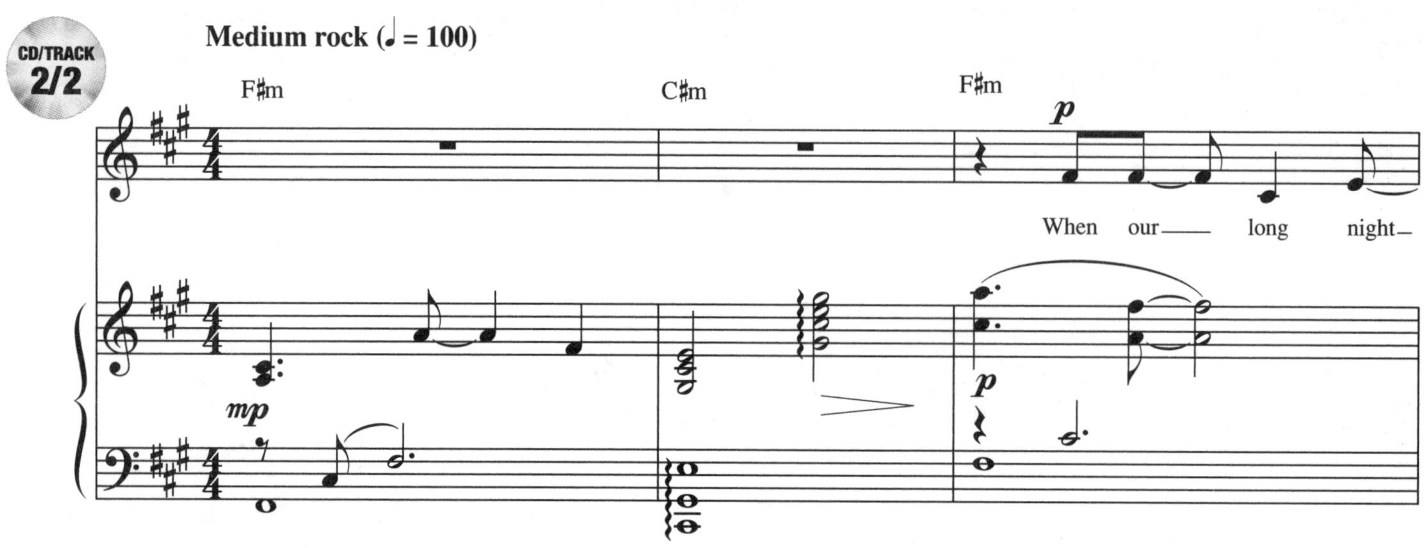

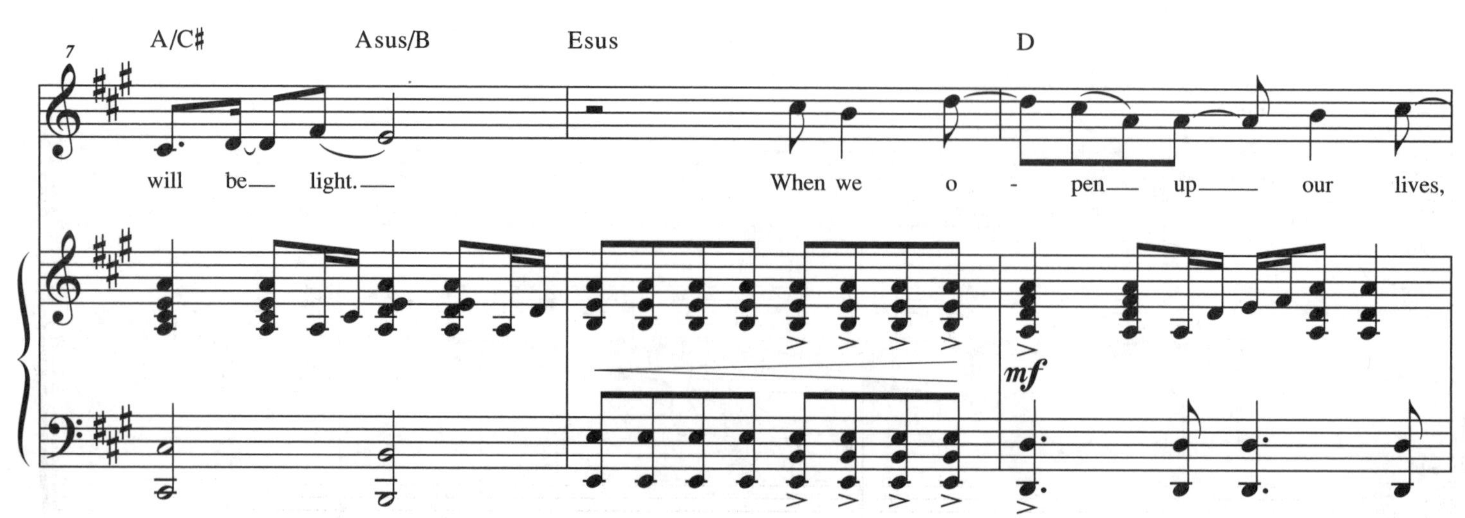

Light - 2 - 1
34277

10
F♯m
D
Bm7
— sons and daugh - ters, — hus - bands, wives — and fight — that fight,
13
Esus
E
D
A
B7
— There will — be light, — there will be light, -
16
B/D♯
B/F♯
B/D♯
B
D(add9)
there will be light. —
19
D
molto rit.
A
There will be light.
f
molto rit.
8va
sfz

A LITTLE BIT IN LOVE

(from "Wonderful Town")

Lyrics by
BETTY COMDEN and ADOLPH GREEN

Music by
LEONARD BERNSTEIN

9
C+(maj7)
C7
F
sub.
p
Dm
Gm7
C7/E
love, then it's love - ly!
Mm,
It's so nice to be a - live
When you
12
F
Dm
Gm7
A
meet some - one
who be - witch - es you.
Will he
14
Dm
freely
F+/C♯
Dm/C
G7sus
G7(♭5)
in tempo
F/C
be my all,
or did I just fall a lit - tle bit,
a
17
Gm/C
B♭/C
C
F6
lit - tle bit in love.
pp

A LITTLE BRAINS, A LITTLE TALENT

(from "Damn Yankees")

Words and Music by
RICHARD ADLER and JERRY ROSS

CD/TRACK 2/4

Jump tempo (in 4) (♩ = 144–152)

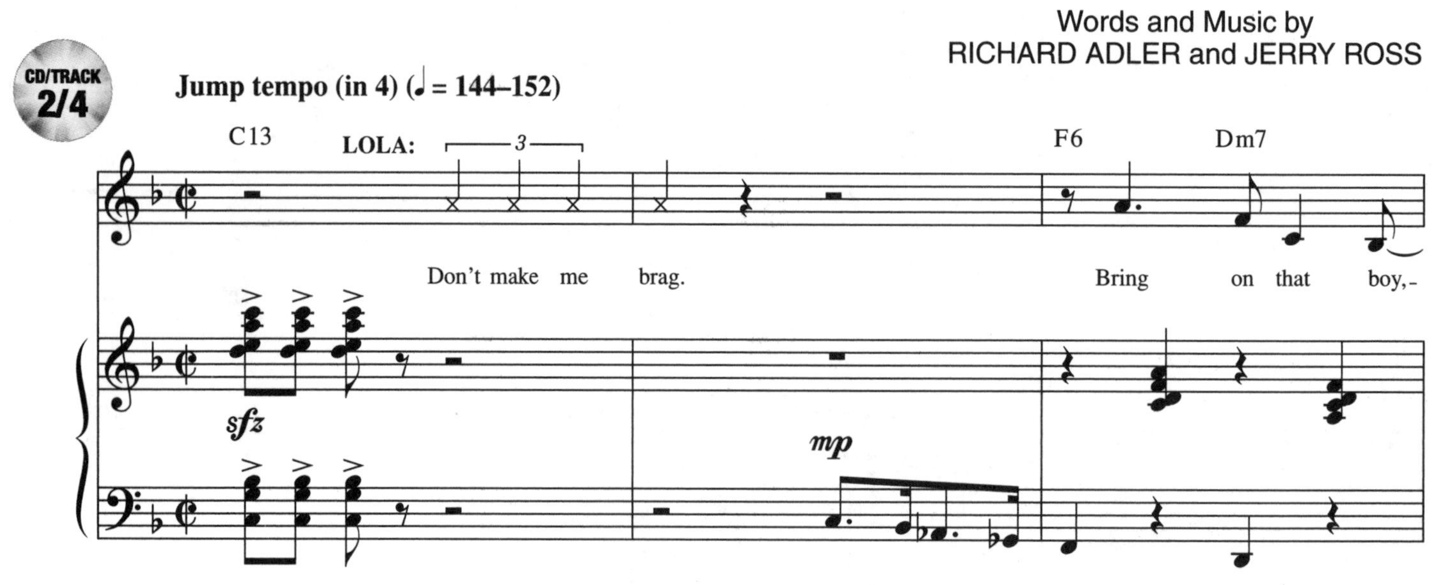

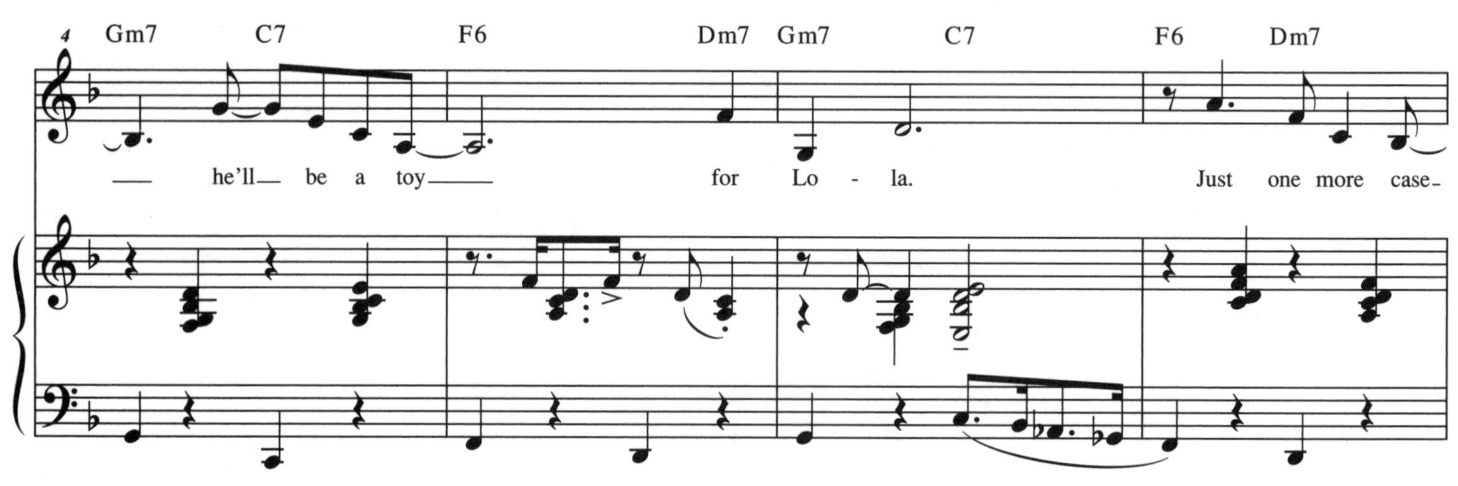

F7
Eb9
Db9
Same as with an - y man, I'll use the stand - ard pat - ter
15
F6/C
D7
plus a lit - tle this - a,
and a lit - tle that - a,
f
18
Db9
C7
Gb9
with an em - pha - sis on the...
21
F6
lat - ter!
ff
sffz

LOOK TO THE RAINBOW

(from "Finian's Rainbow")

Words by
E. Y. HARBURG

Music by
BURTON LANE

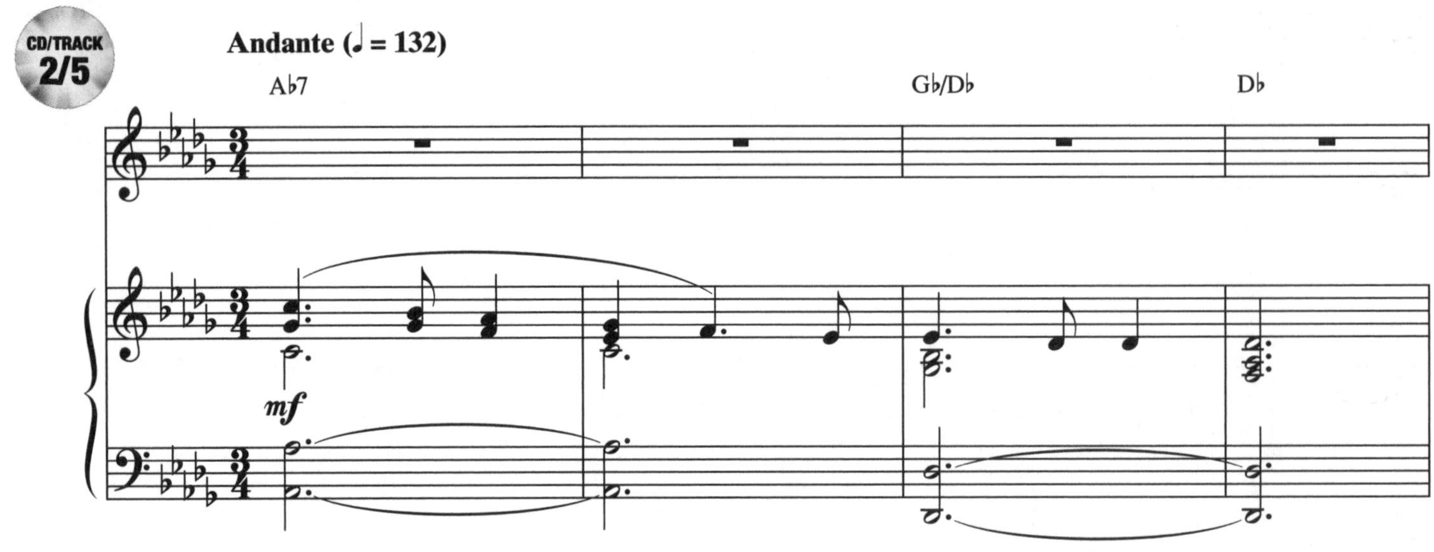

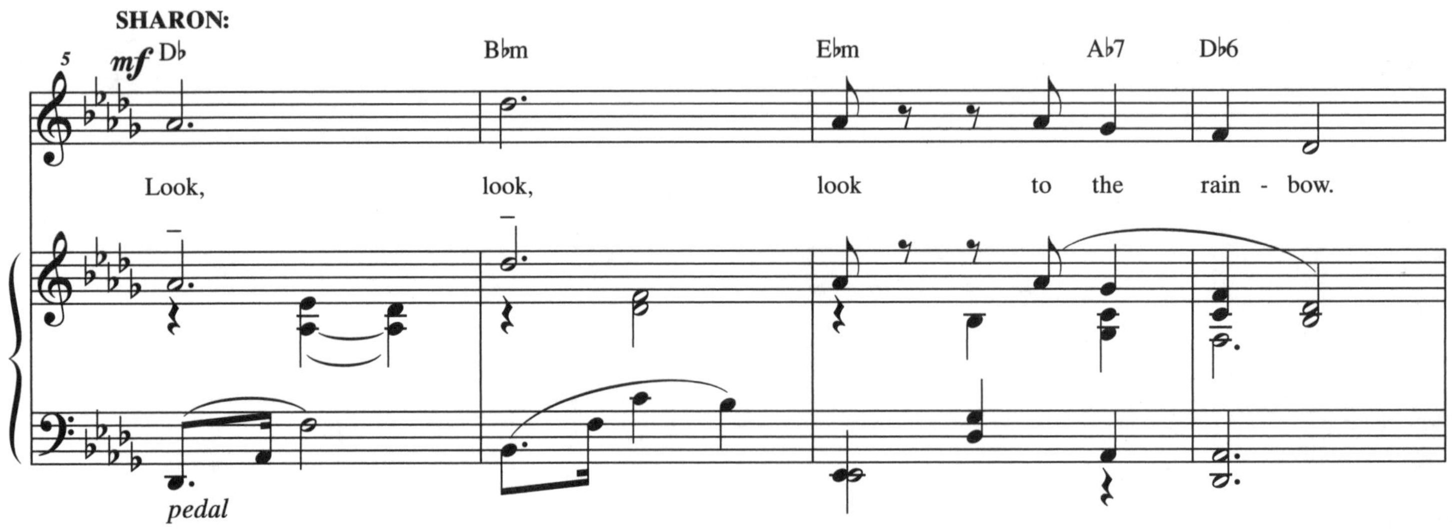

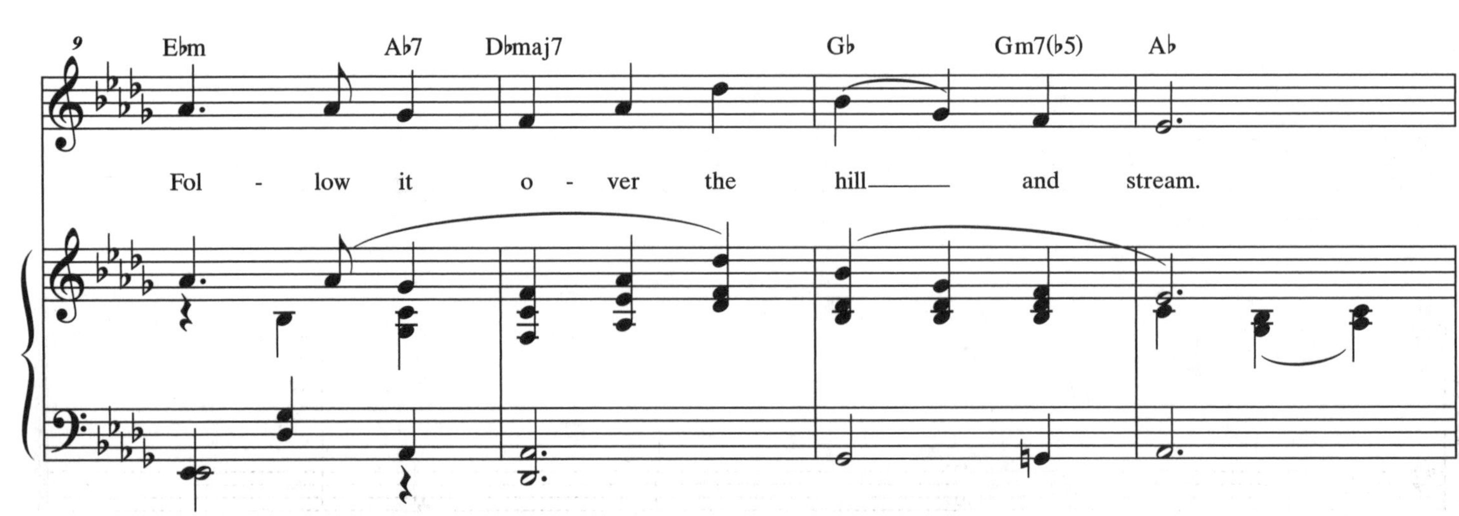

13
D♭
B♭m
E♭m
A♭7
D♭6
Look, look, look to the rain - bow.
pedal
17
G♭
A♭
A♭7
D♭
Fol - low the fel - low who fol - lows a dream.
21
G♭
D♭/A♭
E♭m7
A♭7
D♭
Fol - low the fel - low, fol - low the fel - low.
25
G♭6
pp
Fm/A♭
A♭7
D♭
Fol - low the fel - low who fol - lows a dream.
rit.
pp

LOVE WHO YOU LOVE (REPRISE)

(from "A Man of No Importance")

Lyrics by
LYNN AHRENS

Music by
STEPHEN FLAHERTY

19
D♭ D♭/E♭ Fm9 Cm
mf
hard some - times, and their words can cut so deep. Choose the one you
mf
23
D♭maj9 E♭ Fm9 Fm Cm
choose, love, and don't lose a mo - ment's sleep. Who can tell you
27
D♭maj9 D♭/E♭ C/E B♭m/F Fm
cresc.
who to want? Who can tell you what you were des - tined to
cresc.
31
B♭sus B♭ D♭maj7 D♭/F E♭sus E♭ A♭
decresc.
p poco rit.
be? Take it from me...
decresc.
p poco rit.

LOVELY

(from "A Funny Thing Happened on the Way to the Forum")

Music and Lyrics by
STEPHEN SONDHEIM

21
shame
I can nei-ther sew, nor cook, nor read or write my
25
rall.
a tempo
name.
But I'm ha - py
Mere-ly be-ing love - ly,
rall.
a tempo
30
for there's one thing love-li-ness can do:
It's a
35
gift for me to share with you.
3
p
slowly
f

MAMA WHO BORE ME

(from "Spring Awakening")

Lyrics by
STEVEN SATER

Music by
DUNCAN SHEIK

9 G(add9)/B
D(add9)
A
F(add9)/C
Ma - ma who gave me no way to han - dle things, who
11 G(add9)/B
D(add9)
A
F(add9)/C
made me so bad. Ma - ma, the weep - ing,
13 G(add9)/B
D
F(add9)/C
Ma - ma, the an - gels. No sleep in Heav - en
15 G/B
Asus
rit.
A
or Beth - le - hem.
rit.

MAMA WHO BORE ME (REPRISE)

(from "Spring Awakening")

Lyrics by
STEVEN SATER

Music by
DUNCAN SHEIK

CD/TRACK 2/9

E C(add9) D(add9) A
f
No sleep in Heaven, or Bethlehem. Some
C(add9) G(add9)/B Asus A C(add9)/G D(add9)/F#
pray that one day Christ will come a'-callin'. They light a candle and
f
Esus E C(add9) G(add9)/B Asus A
hope that it glows. And some just lie there crying for Him to come and find them. But
f
C(add9)/G D(add9)/F# E E7 E7sus E7(no3rd)
when He comes, they don't know how to go.

MAMMA MIA

(from "Mamma Mia!")

Words and Music by
BENNY ANDERSSON, STIG ANDERSON
and BJORN ULVAEUS

CD/TRACK 2/10

C/G G D/G D D
9
my, my, just how much I've missed ya? Yes, I've been bro -
A/C♯ Bm A6
12
- ken - heart - ed, blue since the day we part - ed.
G C G Em7 A D
15
Why, why, did I ev - er let you go? Mam-ma Mi - a,
Bm G C G Em7 A D
18
now I real - ly know, my, my, I should not have let you go.

THE MAN I LOVE

(from "Strike Up the Band"–1927)

Music and Lyrics by
GEORGE GERSHWIN and IRA GERSHWIN

CD/TRACK 2/11

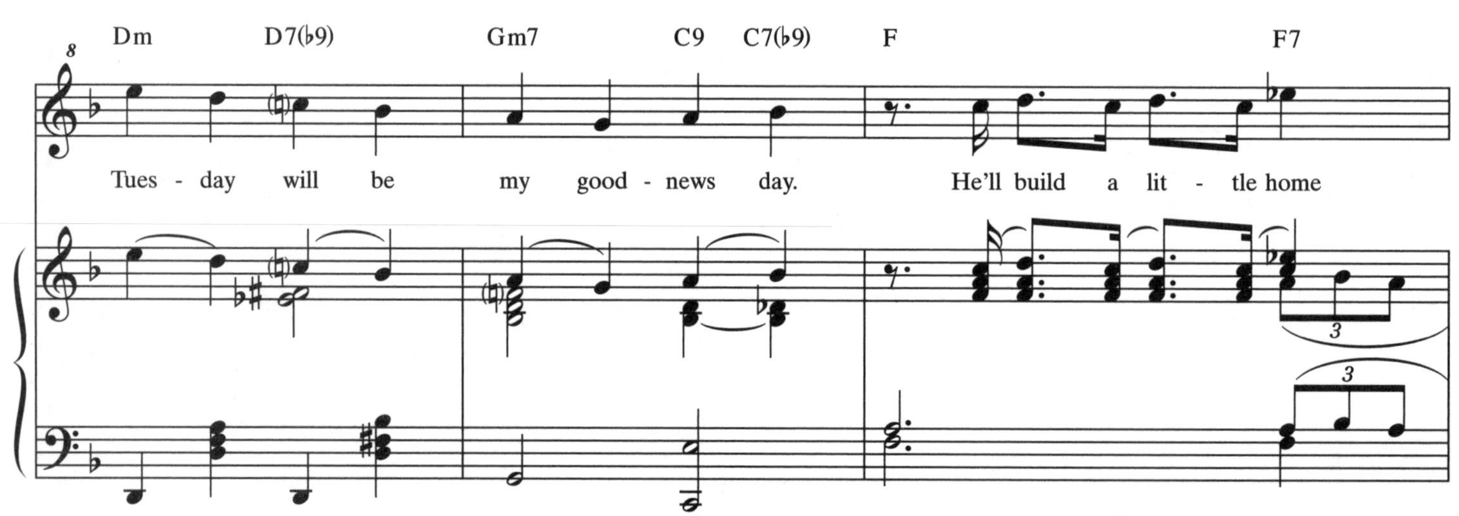

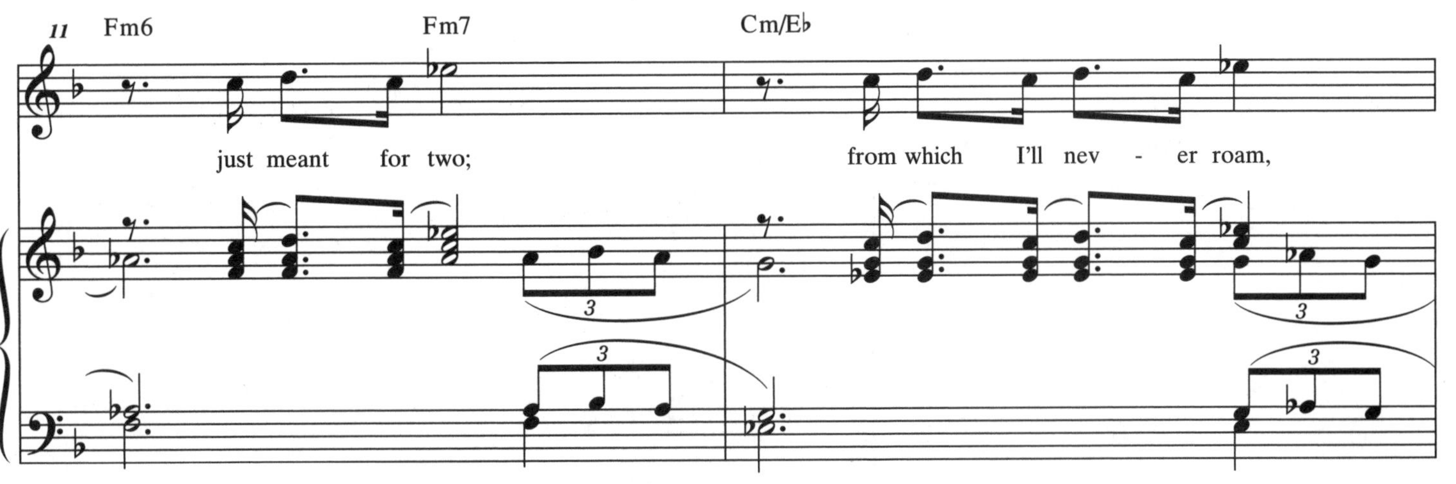
11
Fm6
Fm7
Cm/E♭
just meant for two;
from which I'll nev - er roam,
3
3
3
3

13
B♭+/D
Gm7(♭5)
who would? Would you?
And so, all else a - bove,
3
3
3
3

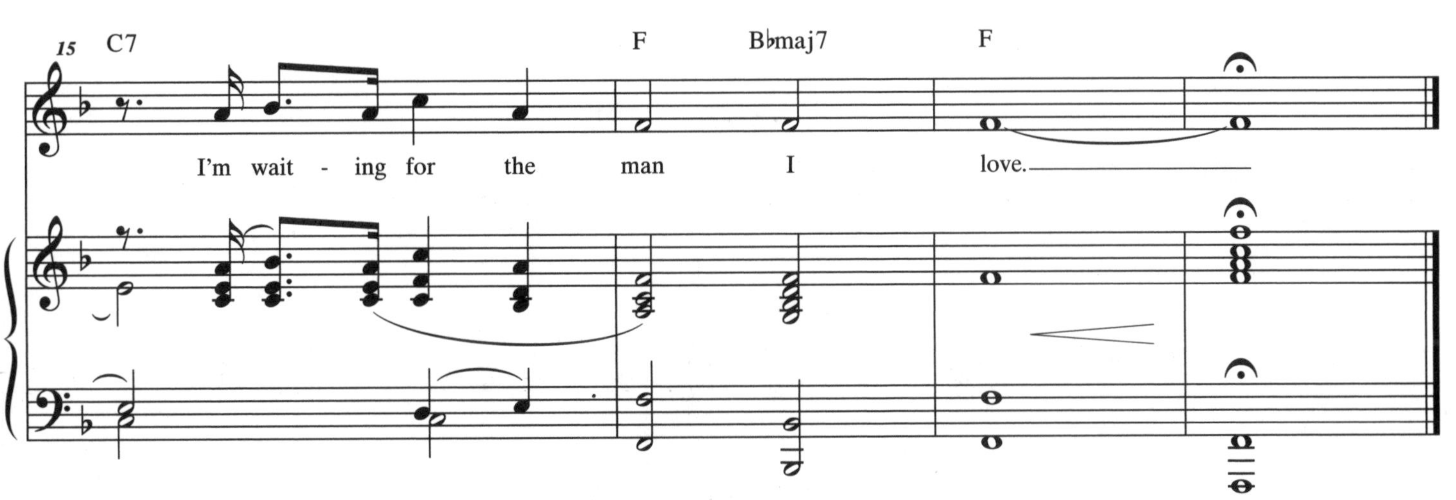
15
C7
F
B♭maj7
F
I'm wait - ing for the man I love.

MIRA

(from "Carnival")

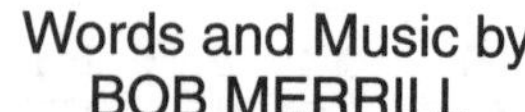

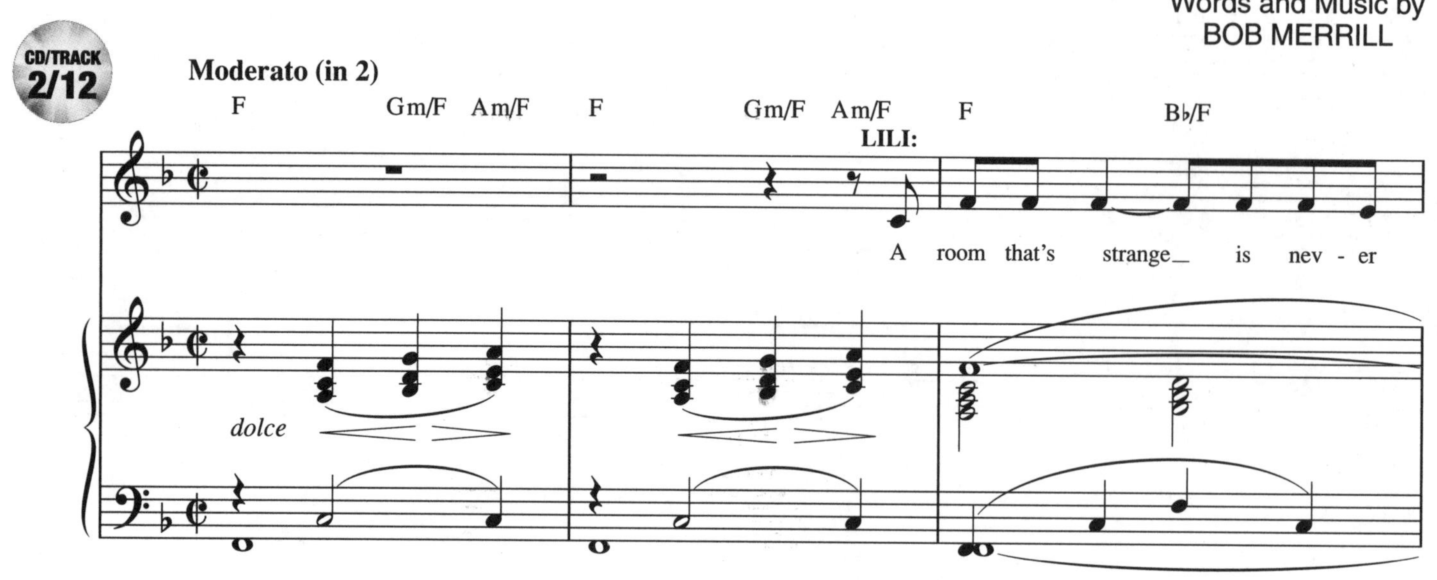

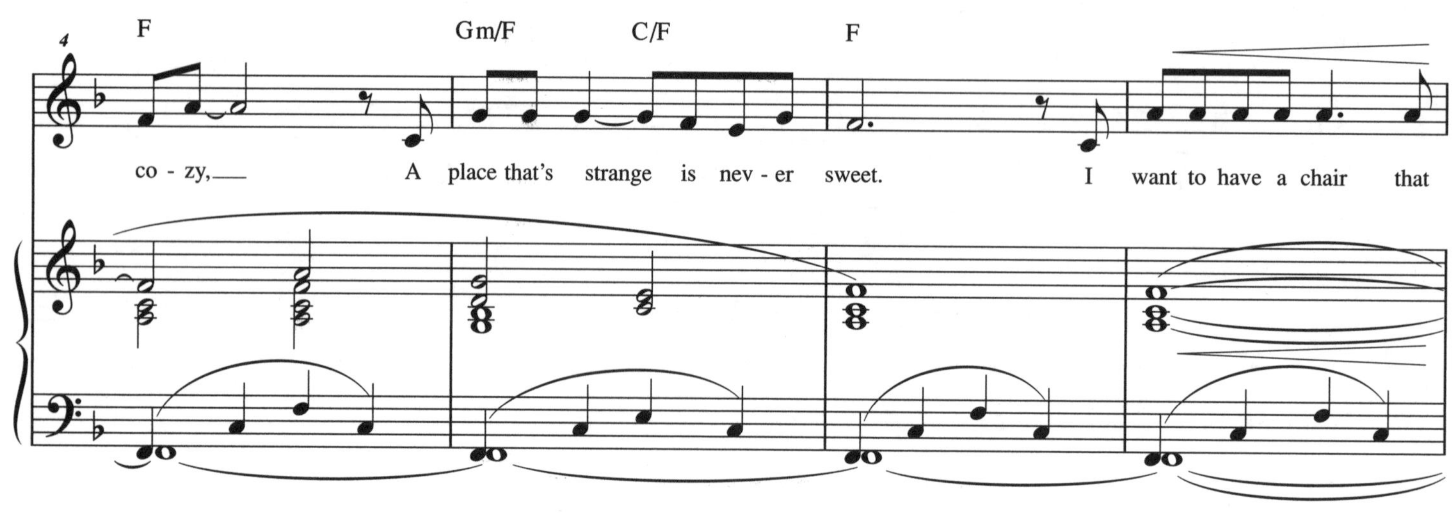

12
F/A
B♭
Gm7
C7
F
pp
Mi - ra now, And there's no turn - ing back. I have to find a place, I've
pp
Pedal
16
Gm/F
Fmaj7
Gm/F
pp
B♭/F
mp dim.
got to find a place, Where ev - 'ry-thing can be the same. A street that I can know, And
pp
mp dim.
20
Fmaj7
Gm7/F
C7
F
B♭
pp
Am
pla - ces I can go, Where ev - 'ry - bod - y knows my name. Can you im - ag - ine that? Can
pp
24
Gm7
Fmaj7
Gm7
C7
F
you im - ag - ine that? Ev - 'ry - bod - y knew my name!

MUCH MORE
(from "The Fantasticks")

Lyrics by
TOM JONES

Music by
HARVEY SCHMIDT

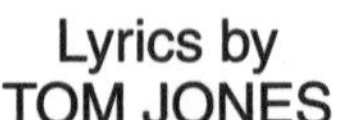

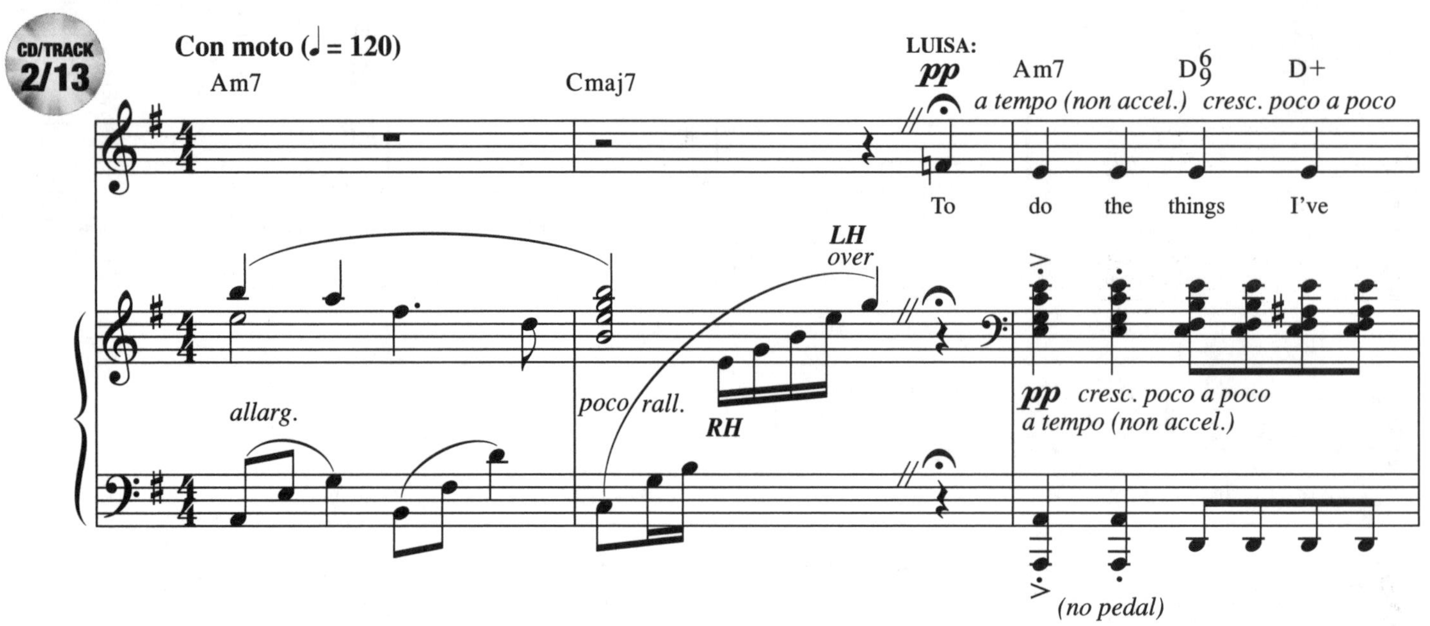

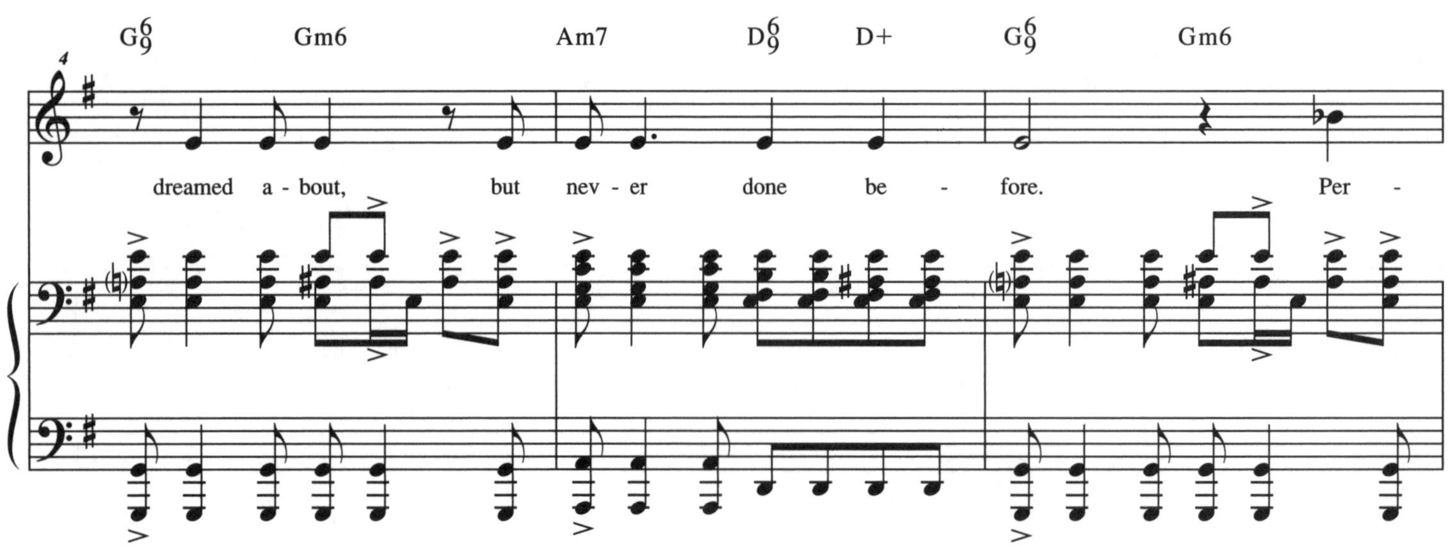

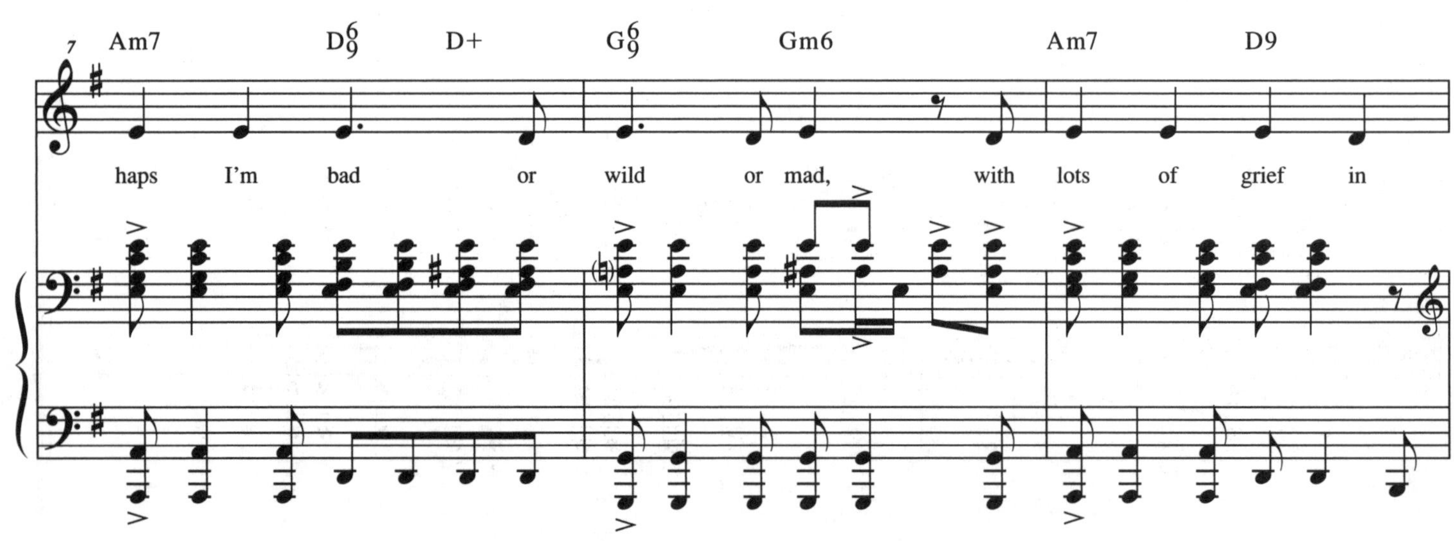

E7sus
E7
Bm
Cmaj7
store, but I want much more than keep - ing house! Much
(with pedal)
Bm
Am7
allarg.
Am/D
Gmaj9
ff a tempo
B♭+(maj7)/E♭
more! Much more! Much more!
allarg.
ff a tempo
Gmaj9
B♭+(maj7)/E♭
Gmaj9
Gmaj9/E♭
Gmaj7
fff poco rit.
fff poco rit.

THE MUSIC THAT MAKES ME DANCE

(from "Funny Girl")

Words by
BOB MERRILL

Music by
JULE STYNE

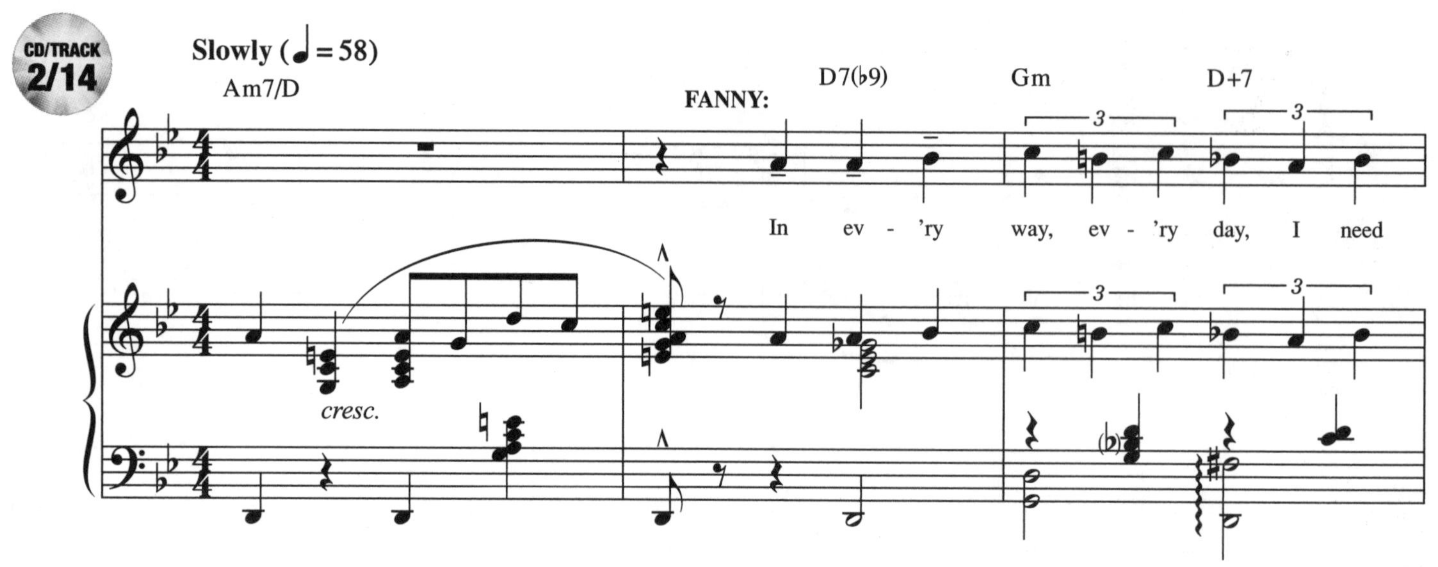

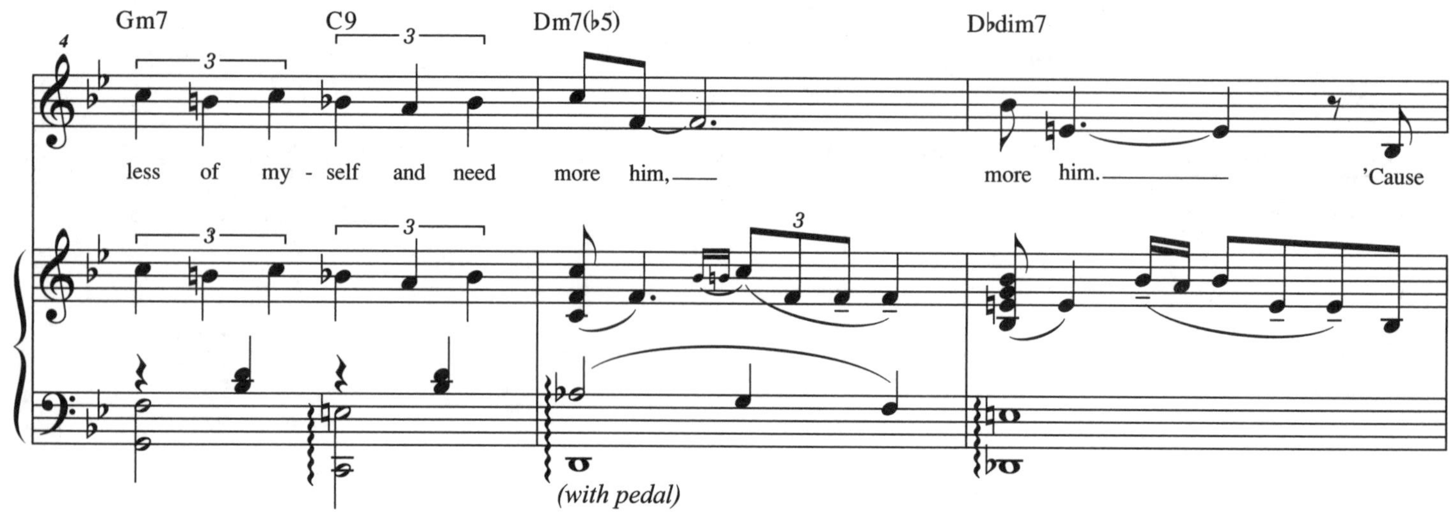

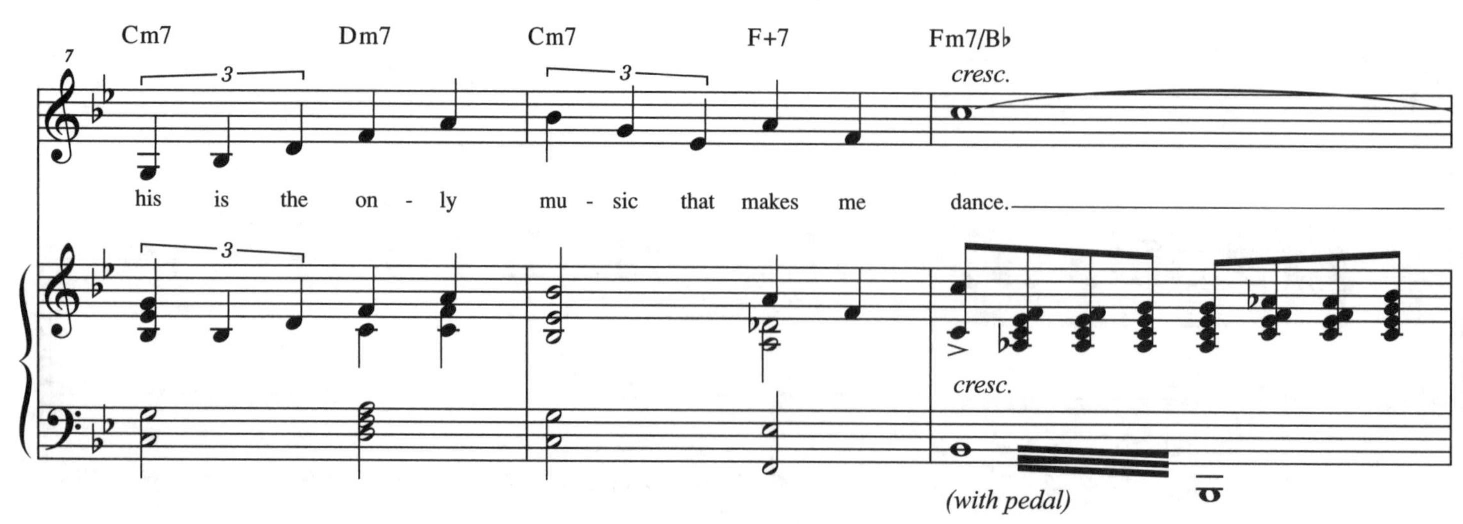

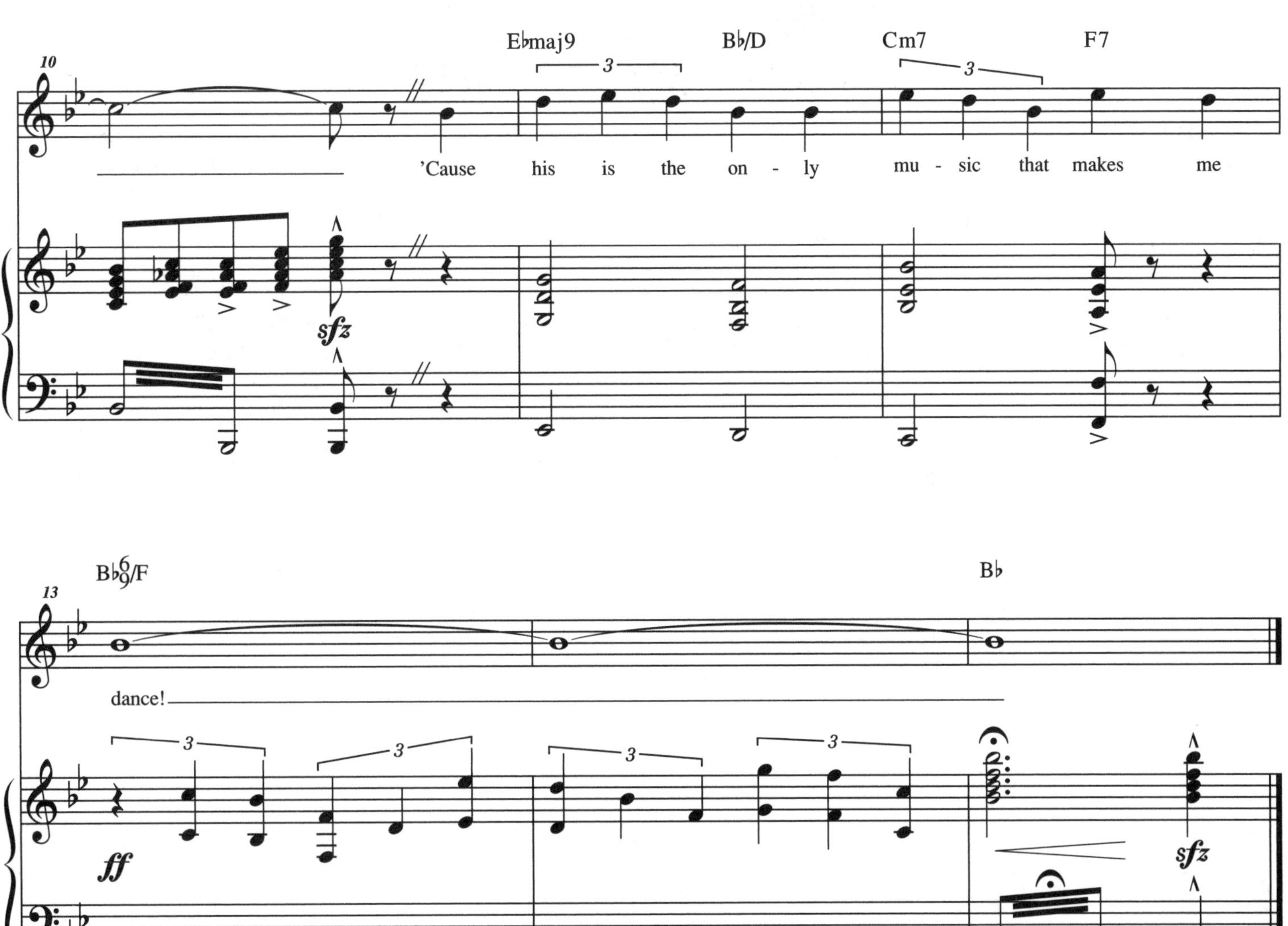

10
E♭maj9
B♭/D
Cm7
F7
3
'Cause his is the on - ly mu - sic that makes me
sfz
13
B♭6/9/F
B♭
dance!
ff
sfz

MY FRIEND, THE DICTIONARY

(from "The 25th Annual Putnam County Spelling Bee")

CD/TRACK 2/15

Moderately bright (𝅗𝅥 = 108)

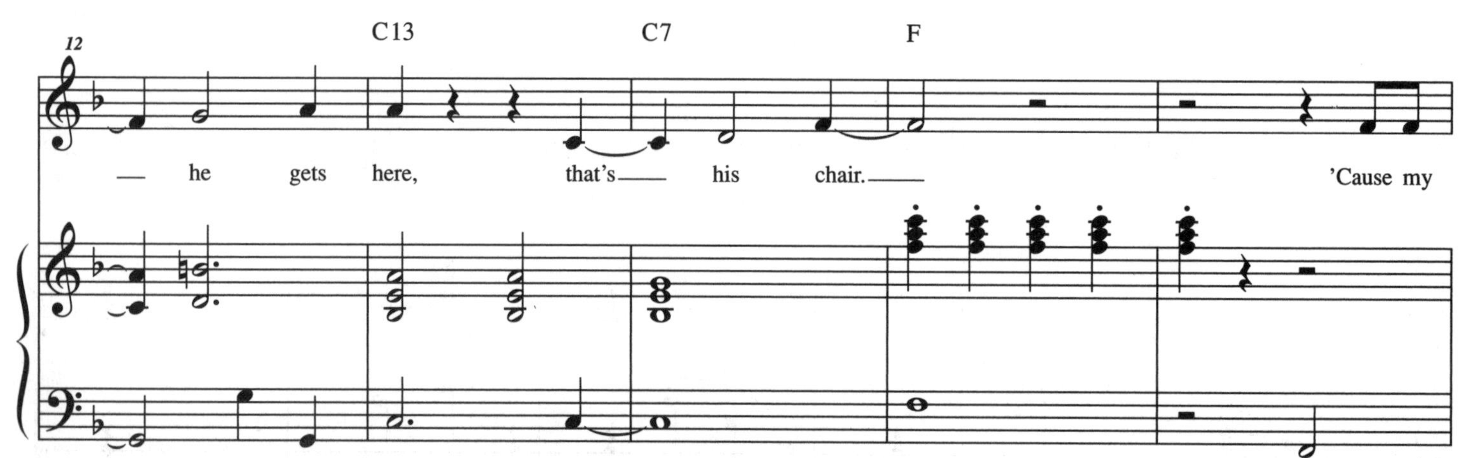

17
A7
Dm
G9
moth - er's in an ash - ram in In - di - a. I saved a chair for her too, but it's
freely with motion
20
C6
Cdim
C
C6
Cdim
C
3
3
3
mere - ly sym - bol - ic, as dai - ly she cleans - es her - self in the Gan - ges. And I
22
F
a tempo
Am7(♭5)
B♭(add9)
Dm/A
3
3
live in a house where there's an o - ver - sized dic - tion -
a tempo
25
Gm7(♭5)
F/C
C9
E♭
C
F
- ar - y that I read as a girl on the toi - let.

MY FUNNY VALENTINE
(from "Babes in Arms")

Words by
LORENZ HART

Music by
RICHARD RODGERS

CD/TRACK
2/16

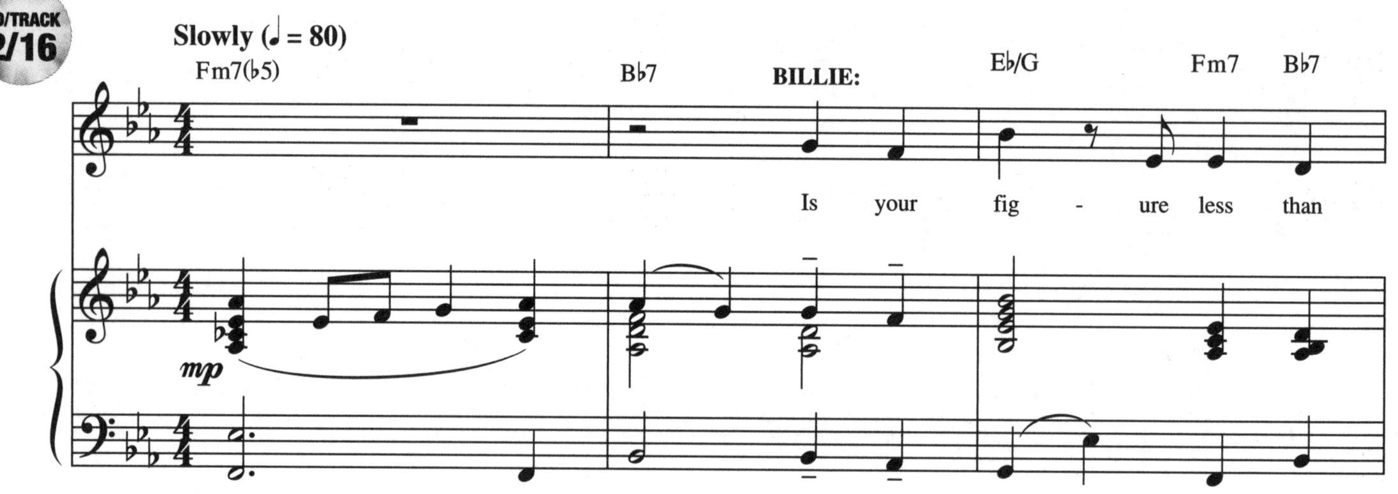

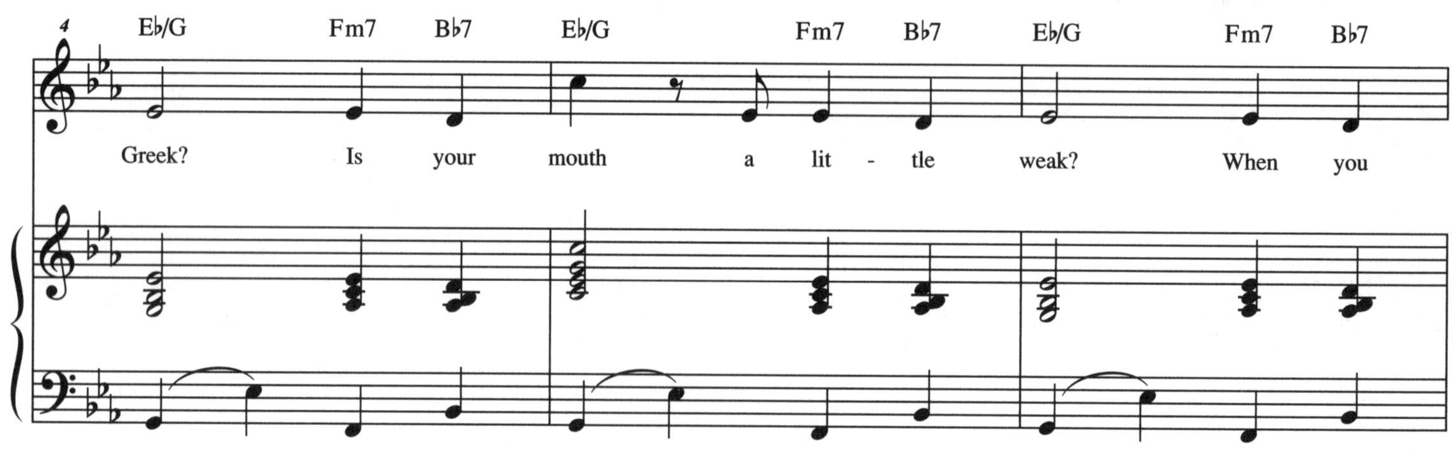

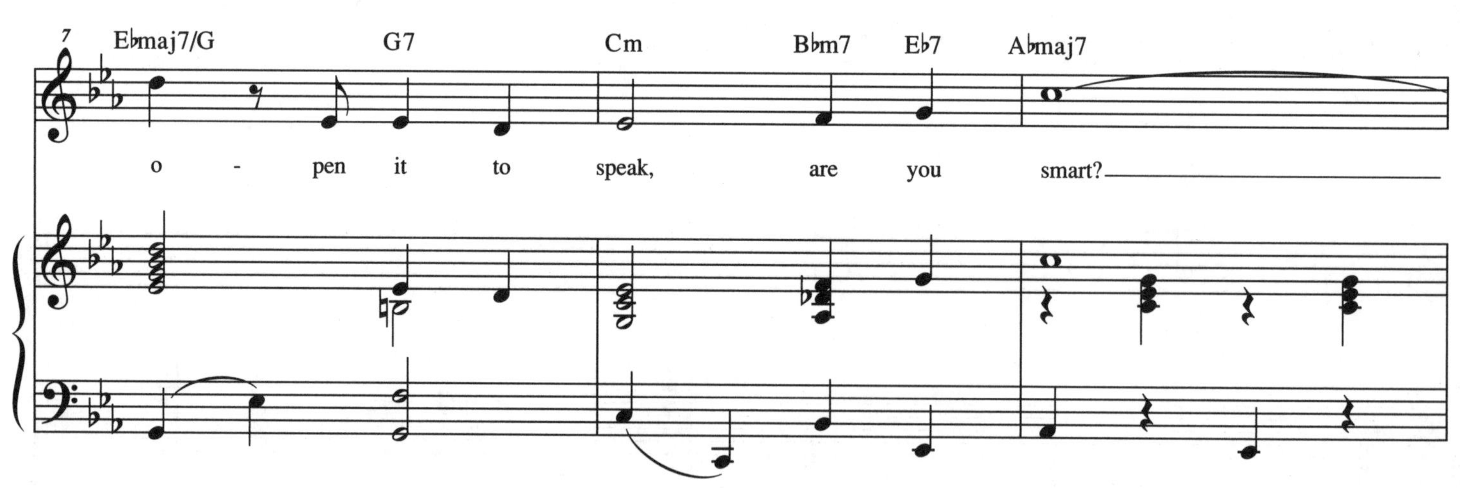

10
A♭7(♯11)
G7
Cm
Cm(maj7)
But don't change a hair for me,
13
Cm7
Cm6
A♭maj7
Not if you care for me. Stay, lit - tle
16
A♭7(♯11)
G7
Cm
B♭m7
E♭7
Val - en - tine, stay!
19
A♭
slower
A♭/G
Fm7
B♭7
E♭6/9
Each day is Val - en - tine's Day.
pp
slower

MY HEART BELONGS TO DADDY

(from "Leave It To Me")

Words and Music by
COLE PORTER

CD/TRACK 2/17

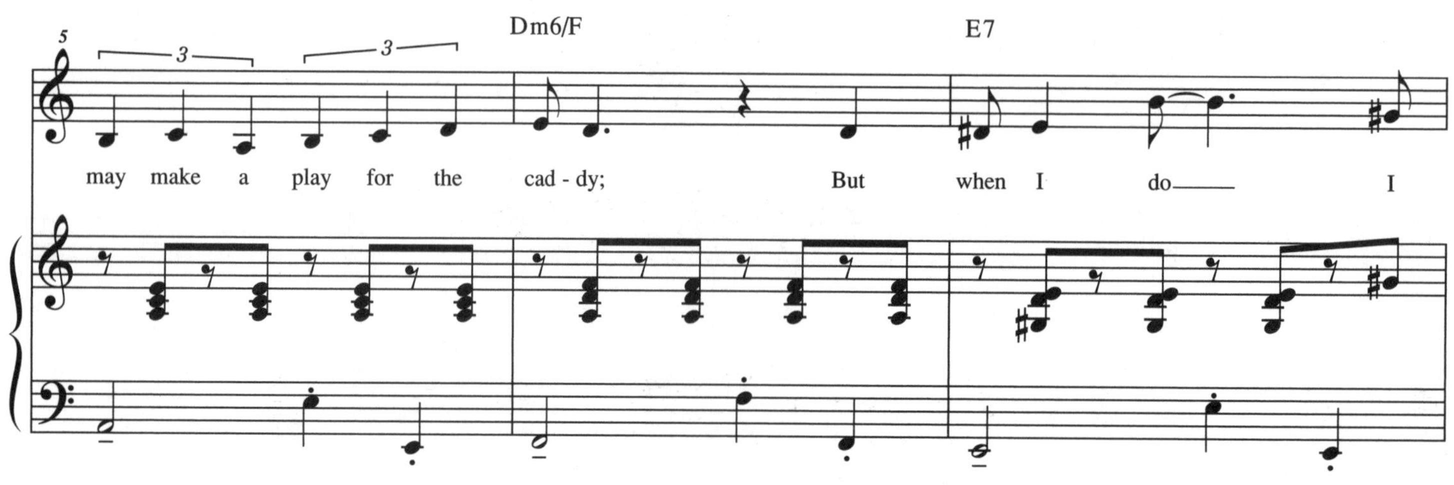

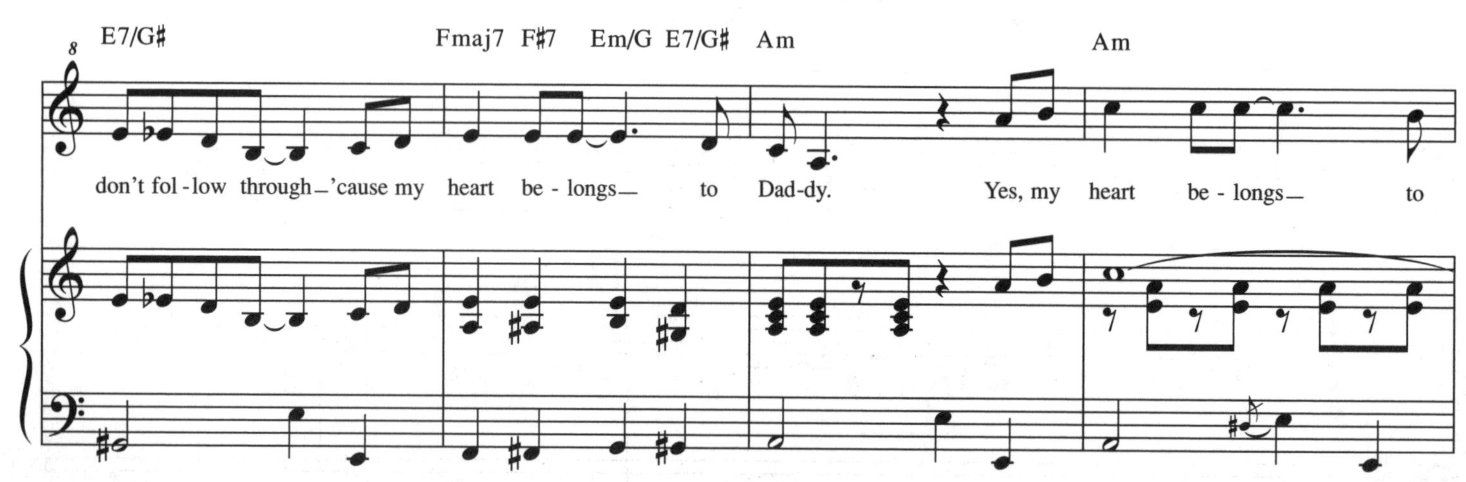

12
E7/G♯
Dad - dy, so I sim - ply could - n't be bad. Yes, my
15
E7(♭9)
A
heart be - longs— to Dad - dy, Da - da, da - da - da, da - da - da - ad! So I
19
A7
D
want to warn— you lad-die, though I know you're per - fect - ly swell, that my
23
Dm
A/C♯
E7sus/B
E7
Am
heart be - longs— to Dad - dy— 'cause my Dad - dy, he treats it so well.

MY HEART STOOD STILL

(from "A Connecticut Yankee")

Words by
LORENZ HART

Music by
RICHARD RODGERS

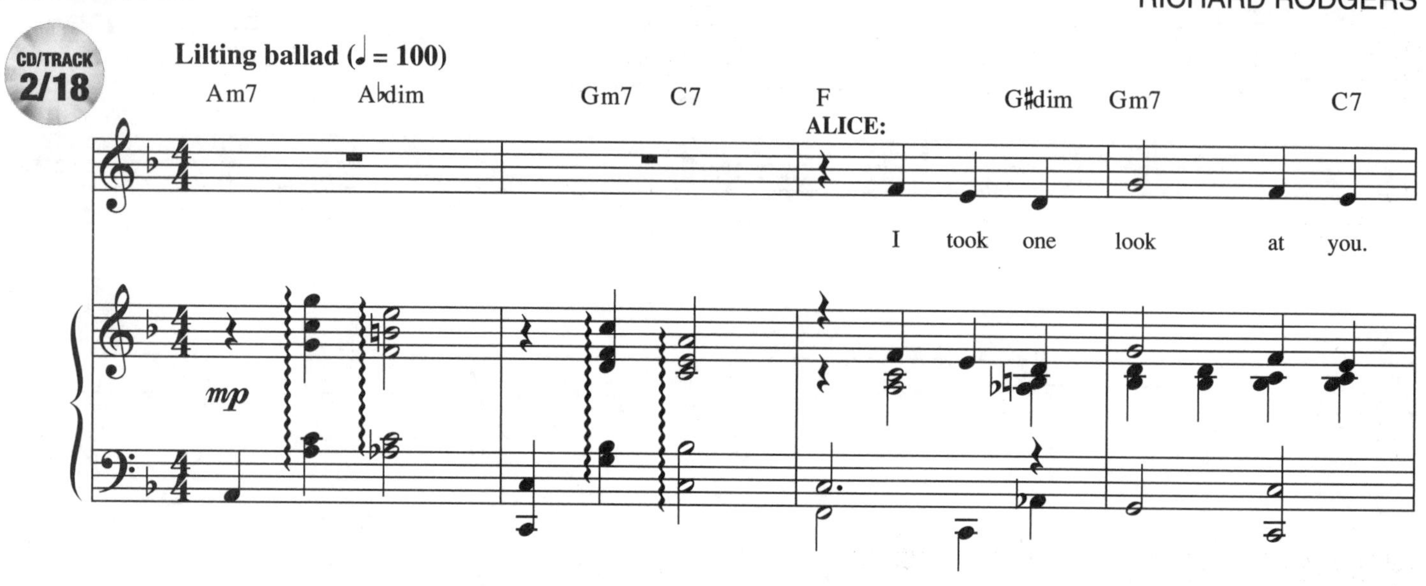

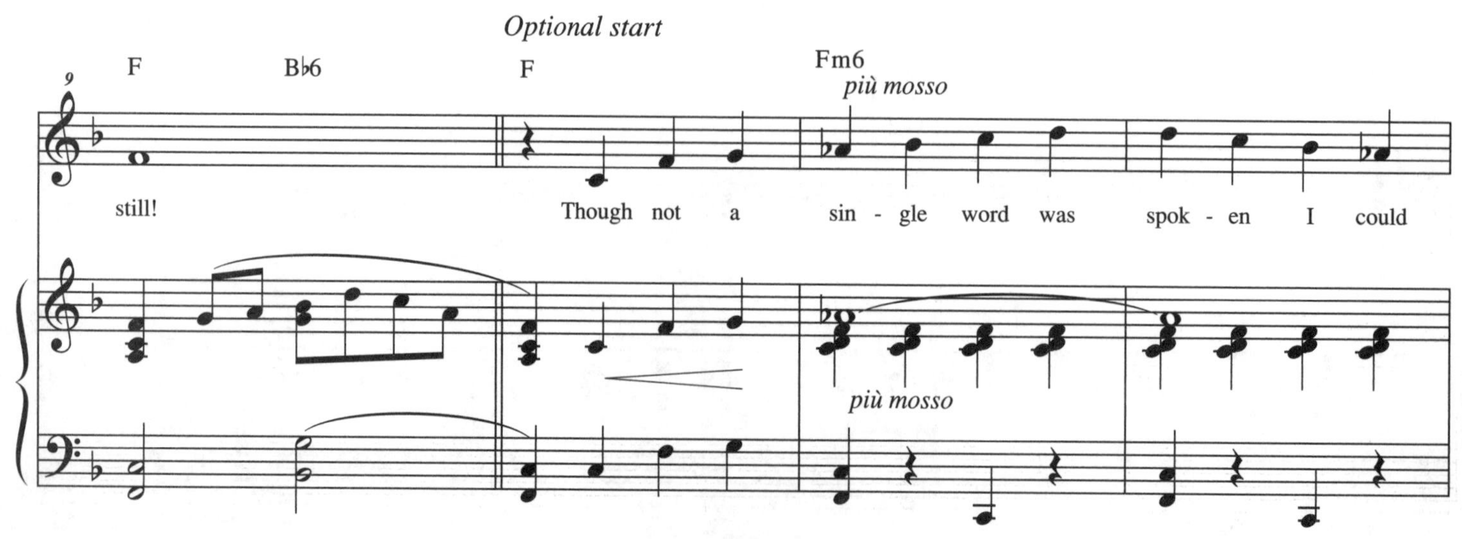

13
C+ C Dm7(♭5) G7
tell you knew, that un - felt clasp of hands told me so
17
C+7 C7 F G♯dim Gm7 C7
a tempo
well you knew. I nev - er lived at all
rall.
a tempo
21
F F+ B♭maj7 B♭maj7/A Gm7
cresc.
un - til the thrill of that mo - ment when my
cresc.
24
F/C C7 F B♭6 F
dim.
heart stood still.
8va
dim.

THE NEW GIRL IN TOWN

(from "Hairspray: The Movie")

Lyrics by
SCOTT WITTMAN and
MARC SHAIMAN

Music by
MARC SHAIMAN

CD/TRACK 2/19

Moderately fast rock & roll (♩ = 126)

10
A♭
G♭6
D♭
We don't know what to do 'bout the new girl in town.
13
D♭7
G♭
D♭
G♭
She's hip. So cool. I'm gon - na get her
17
D♭
G♭
D♭
af - ter school! And yet, we'd like to be like her, 'cause
20
E♭7
A♭
E♭m/G♭
A♭/F
A♭/E♭
D♭
she's the kit - ten that the cats pre - fer.

NOT FOR THE LIFE OF ME

(from "Thoroughly Modern Millie")

Lyrics by
DICK SCANLAN

Music by
JEANINE TESORI

CD/TRACK 2/20

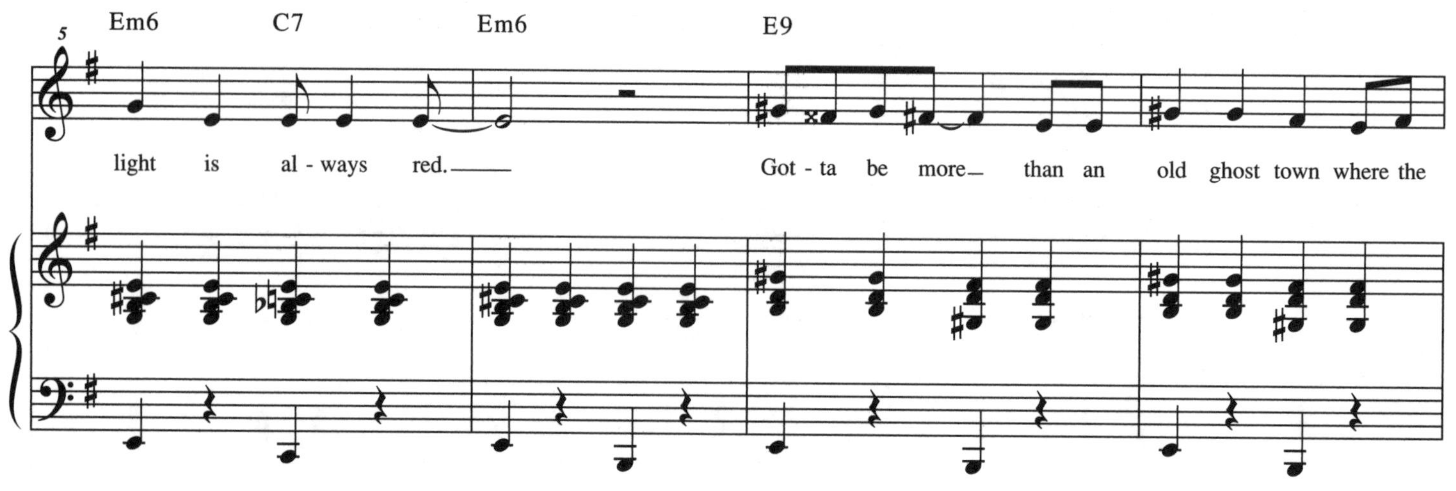

13
E♭9
Cm7(♭5)
A♭7
D♭7
- be - cause don't you know that where I am ain't where I was.
16
B♭7
E♭7
Cm7(♭5)
F7
B♭7
Not for the life of me.
Boh doh dee oh.
Not for the
21
E♭7
A♭7
D♭
Ddim7
A♭/E♭
E7
life of,
not for the life of,
not for the life
26
E♭9
A♭
B♭
A♭+7
B♭+7
A♭
of me!
L.H.

NOTICE ME HORTON

(from "Seussical the Musical")

Lyrics by
LYNN AHRENS

Music by
STEPHEN FLAHERTY

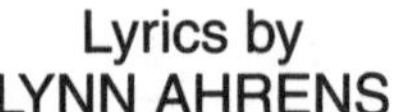

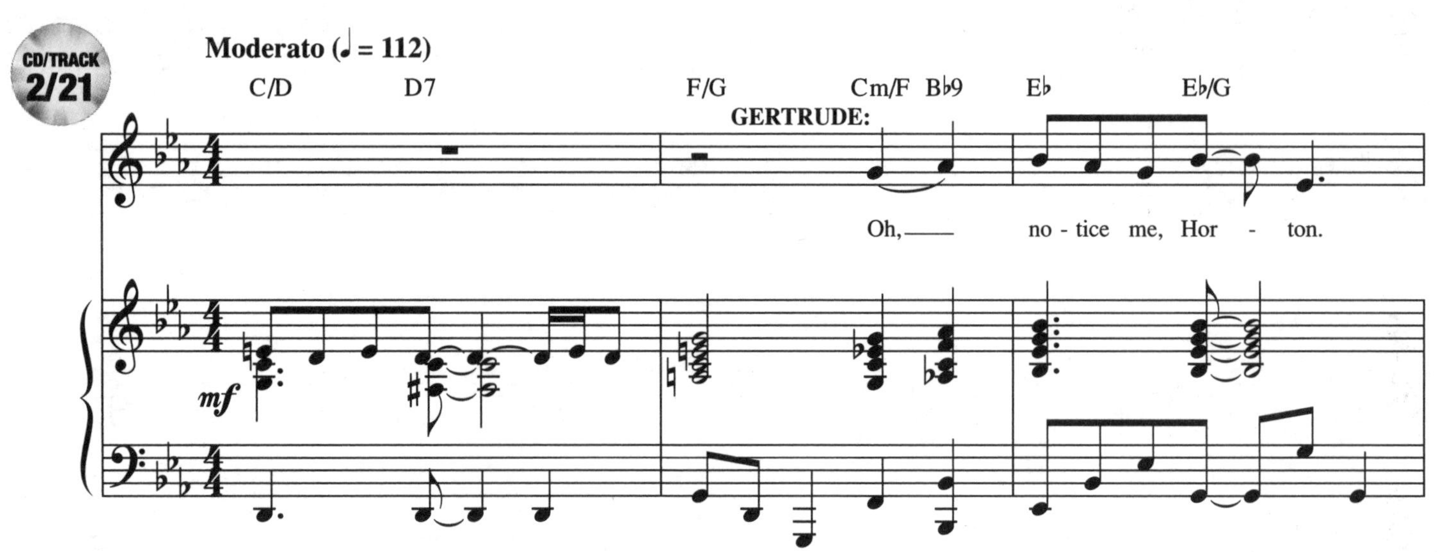

10
A♭(add9)
E♭/G
Cm7
I was just a no - one on - ly yes - ter - day.
f
14
Cm7/F
E♭/B♭
A♭/B♭
D♭/E♭
E♭
D♭/E♭
E♭/D♭
You showed up and showed me some - thing more.
Now
18
C♭(add9)
B♭m7
E♭m7
I've be - come a some - one who has some - one to be - lieve in and to
22
E♭sus/F
Fm7
A♭(add9)/B♭
B♭
be there for...
8va
L.H.

ONCE UPON A DREAM

(from "Jekyll & Hyde")

Lyrics by
LESLIE BRICUSSE

Music by
FRANK WILDHORN

10
Gbsus
Gb
Cb
sent to me. Was it nev - er meant to be?
13
Db
Ddim
Ebm7
Ab7
Are you just a dream? Could we be -
16
Abm9
slowly
- gin a - gain, once up - on a
19
Gb
Db/Cb
Cb
Gb
dream?

ONLY LOVE
(from "The Scarlet Pimpernel")

Words by
NAN KNIGHTON

Music by
FRANK WILDHORN

10
D
D/E
E
A
D
A/C♯
let it re - lease you. Take the chance, it's on - ly love.
13
Bm
A/C♯
D
A
F♯m
Let it come through you slow - ly. O - pen your heart and show me.
15
Bm
rit.
D/E
E7
D/A
A(add9)
Don't be a - fraid, it's on - ly love.
rit.

OUT HERE ON MY OWN

(from "Fame: The Movie")

Lyrics by
LESLEY GORE

Music by
MICHAEL GORE

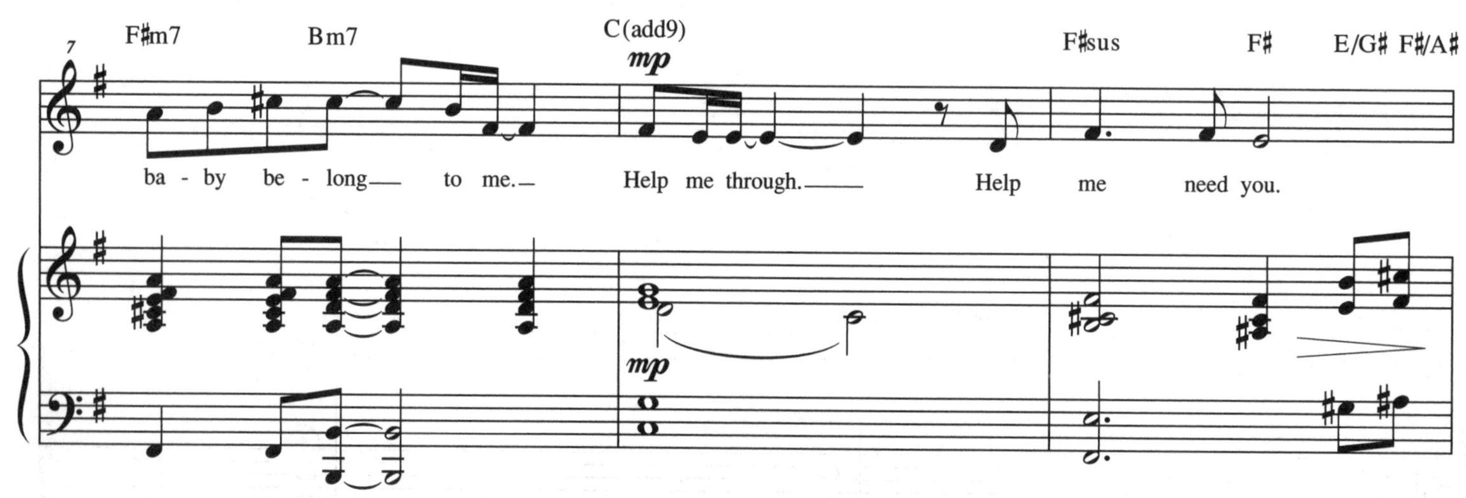

10
C/E
Bm/F♯
Cmaj7
C6
Some - times I won - der where I've been, who I am,
13
G/B
Am9
G/B
do I fit in? I may not win — but I can't be thrown
16
Cmaj7
D7sus
D7
G
out here on my own.
19
D/G
C/G
freely
G
Out — here on my own.
freely

OVER THE RAINBOW

(from "The Wizard of Oz")

Lyrics by
E.Y. HARBURG

Music by
HAROLD ARLEN

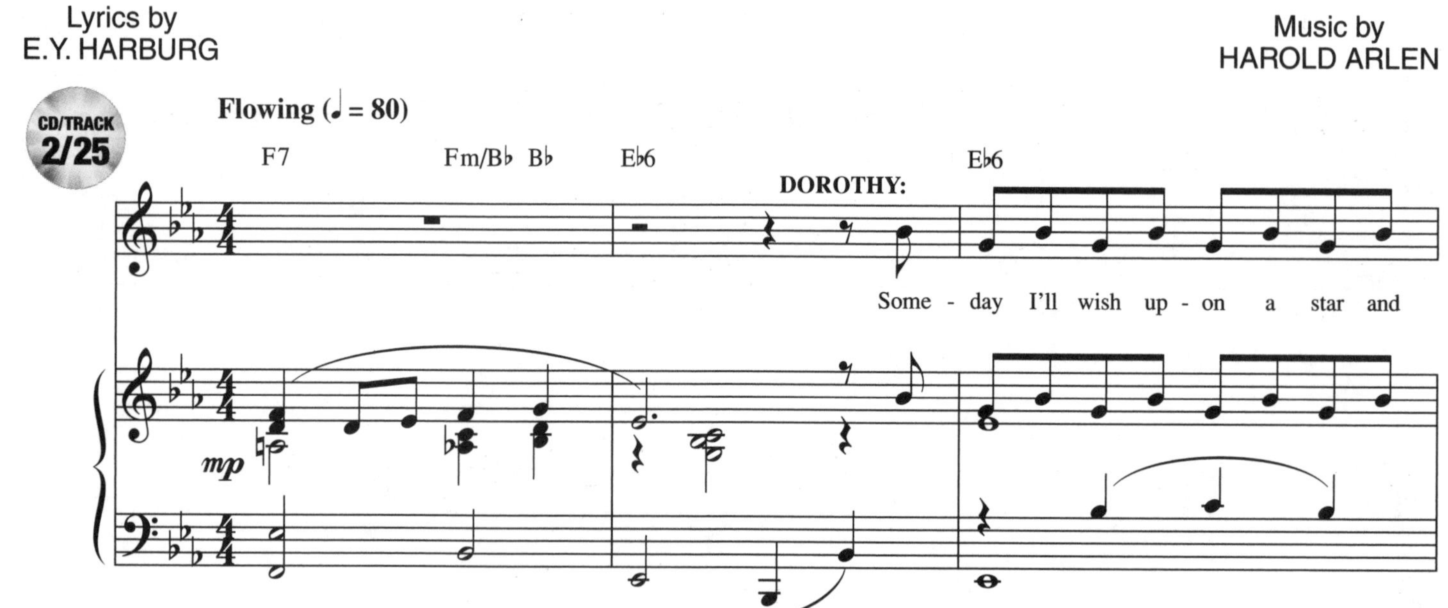

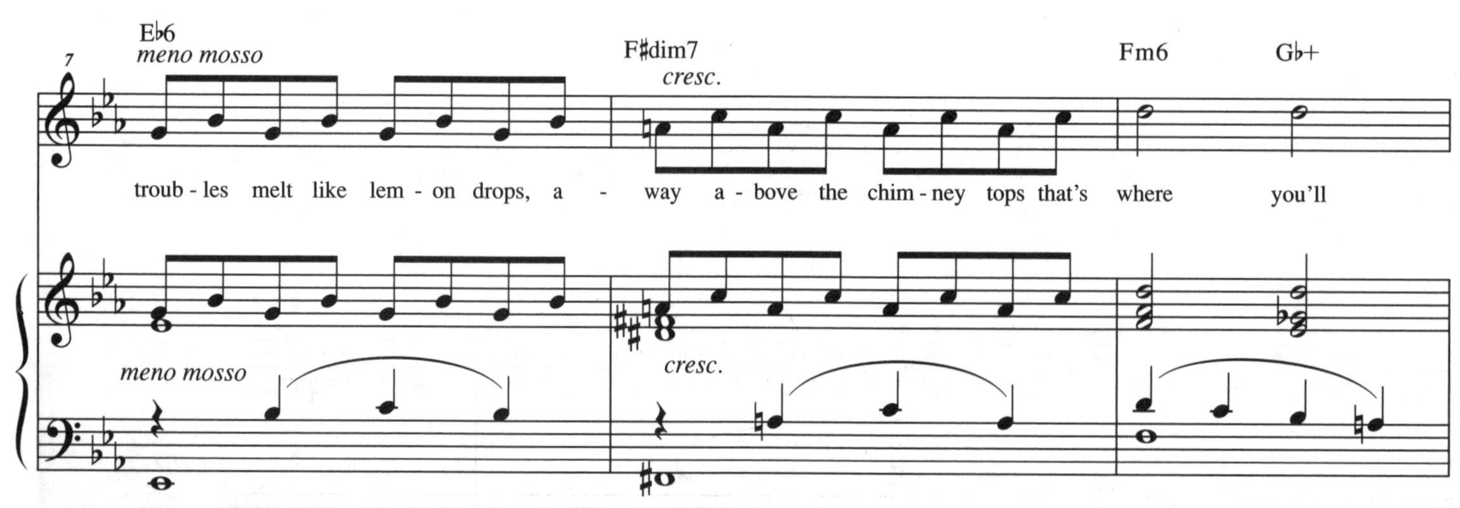

Fm7/B♭ B♭7(♯5) E♭6 Cm7 Gm E♭7 A♭ A♭7
10
dim. slight rall.
mp a tempo
find me. Some - where o - ver the rain - bow blue - birds
dim. slight rall.
mp
a tempo
Gm7 Gdim7 A♭6 A♭m6 E♭/B♭ C7(♭9)
14
fly. Birds fly o - ver the rain - bow,
F7 Fm7/B♭ B♭7 E♭ Fm7 B♭ E♭6
17
why then, oh why can't I? If hap - py lit - tle blue - birds fly be -
Fm7 B♭7 E♭6
20
rit.
yond the rain - bow, why oh why can't I?
rit.
L.H.
ppp

PRINCESS

(from "A Man of No Importance")

Lyrics by
LYNN AHRENS

Music by
STEPHEN FLAHERTY

CD/TRACK 2/26

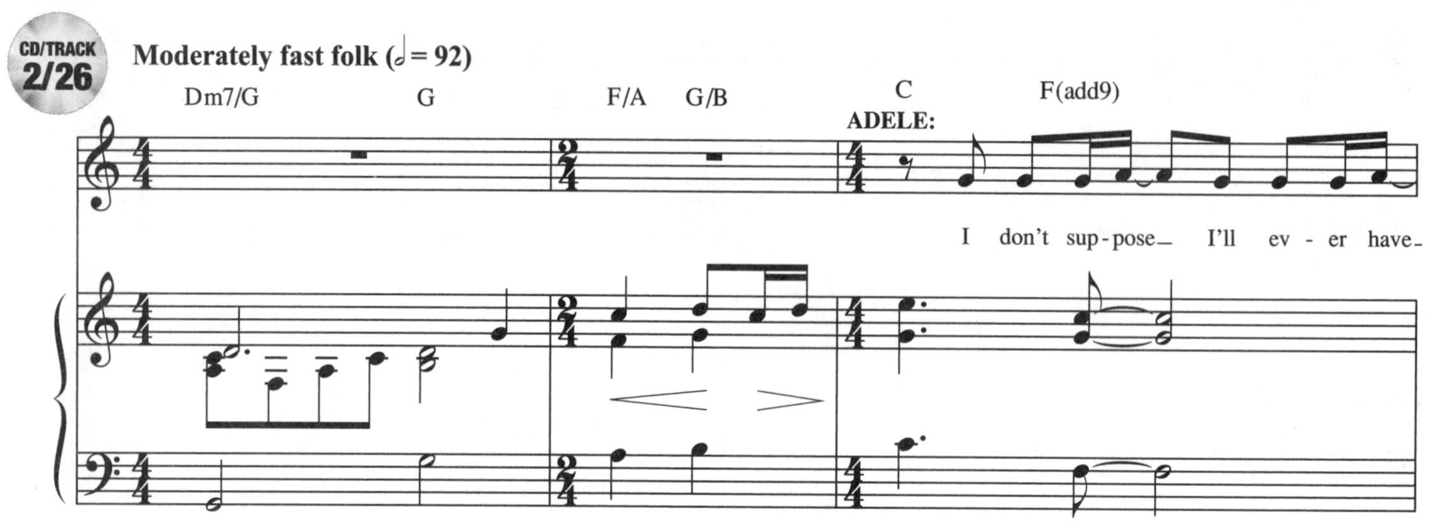

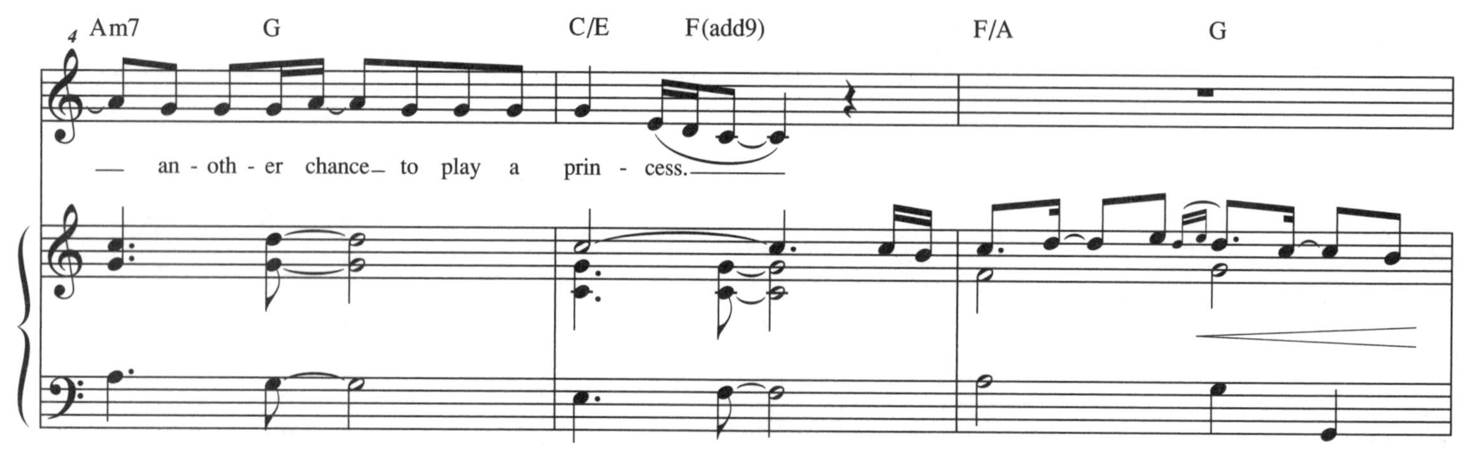

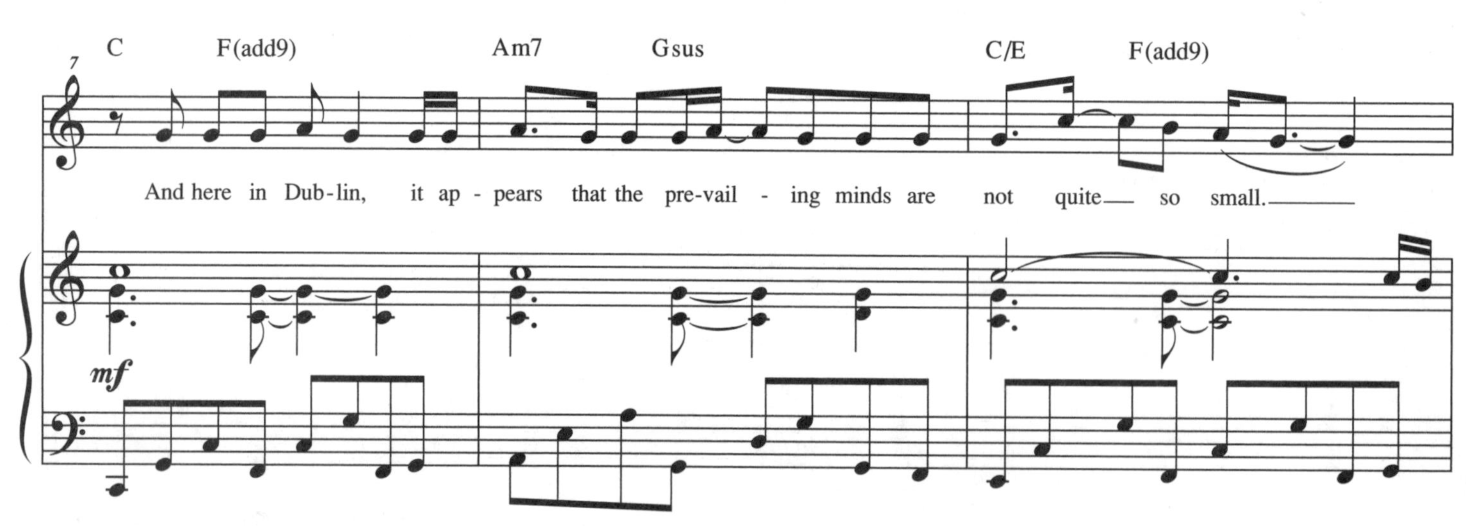

10 F/A G E♭ A♭(add9) Fm7 B♭/D
I swore I would-n't spend my life back in Ros-com-mon. I'd be
13 C/E Am B♭13(♯11)
some - one go - ing some - place they would nev - er dream of,
(wth pedal)
16 C/E F(add9) Am B♭ E7 Am
the on - ly dream - er that Ros - com-mon will be a - ble to re - call.
19 Am7/D D Csus/D G7sus F/A G C
poco rit.
colla voce
a tempo
Seems like Ros-com-mon raised a prin - cess af - ter all.

RAUNCHY

(from "110 in the Shade")

Words by
TOM JONES

Music by
HARVEY SCHMIDT

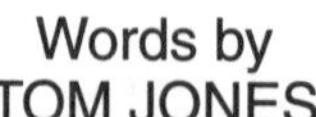

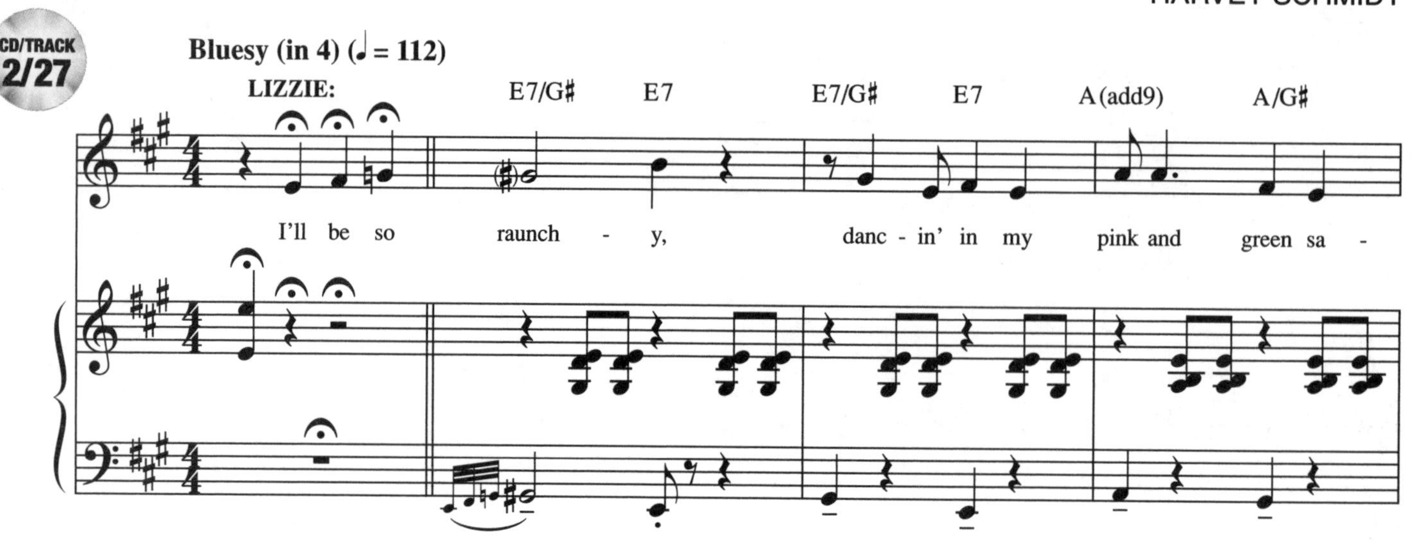

14
D7 D♯dim7 A D D♯dim7 A
men folk see me shim - my by, gon - na break right out in shin - gles, 'cause I'm
Stripper tempo
18
D D♯dim7 A/E F♯+7 B7 Cdim7
guar - an - teed to sat - is - fy. I'm a raunch - y I'm a
rit.
22
C♯m7(♭5) F♯+7(♯9) B9 E7
raunch - y, I'm a raunch - y kind of
26
F♯m7/A F♯m7(♭5)/G F♯m7(♭5) F♯m7/F B9 Bm7/E A7
gal. Raunch - y kind - a gal.

RHODE ISLAND IS FAMOUS FOR YOU

(from "Inside U.S.A.")

Words by
HOWARD DIETZ

Music by
ARTHUR SCHWARTZ

15
Em7 A7(♭9) D7 Am7 D7 D+7 Gmaj7
camp - chair in New Hamp - chair, that's for me. And min-nows
20
Am7 D+7 Gmaj7 Am7 D+7 Gmaj7 Em7 D♯dim7 Em7 A13
come from Min - now - sot - a, coats come from Da - coat-a, but why should you be blue?
25
A+7 A7 Am7(♭5)/E♭ Gmaj7 /D G7 C
For you, you come from Rhode Is - land, and
30
Cm(maj7) G/D Am7 D7 G
lit - tle old Rhode Is - land is fa - mous for you!

ROXIE
(from "Chicago")

Lyrics by
FRED EBB

Music by
JOHN KANDER

CD/TRACK 2/29

12
G6
G♯dim7
Am7
D7
dumb me - chan - ic's wife I'm gon - na be Rox - ie.
G9
15
C6
C7
Who says that mur - der's not an art?
And
19
E♭7(♯11)
G6
A9/C♯
who in case she does - n't hang can say she start - ed with a bang?
23
G
G dim7/D
Am7(♭5)/D
D7
G
(Spoken) "Thank you."
Fox - y, Rox - ie Hart!
3
p

THE SAILOR OF MY DREAMS

(from "Dames At Sea")

Words and Music by
JIM WISE, ROBIN MILLER and
GEORGE HAIMSOHN

CD/TRACK 2/30

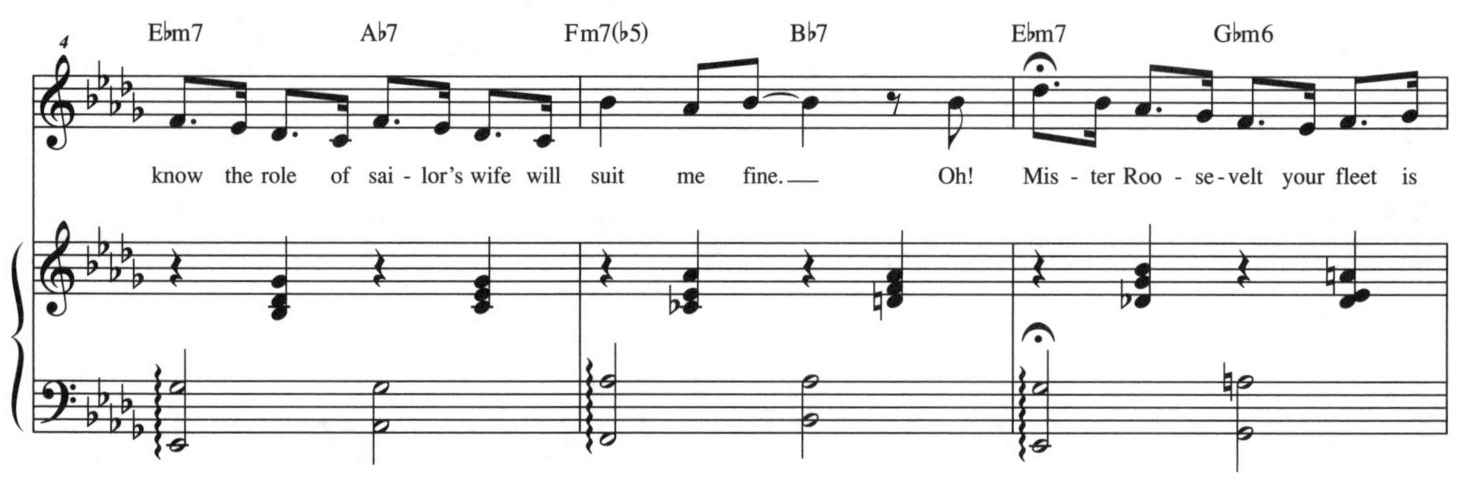

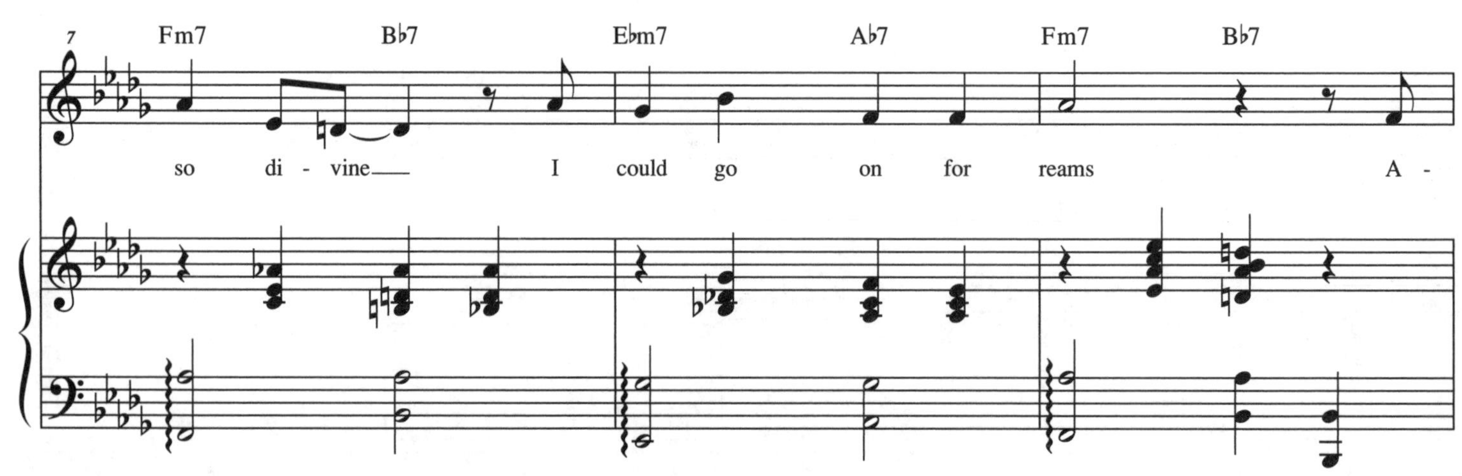

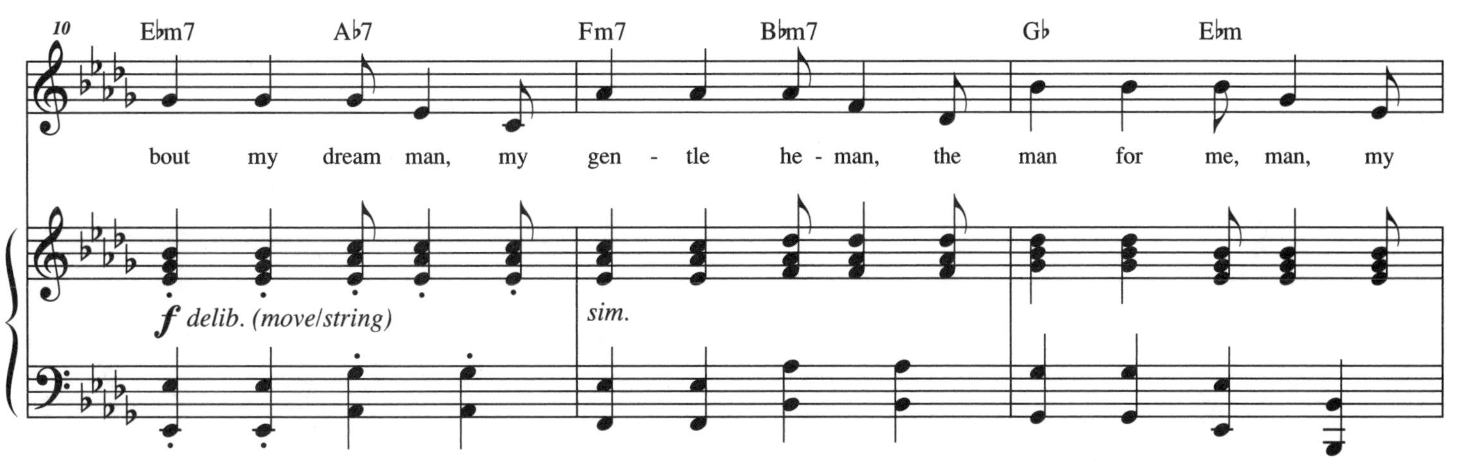
10
E♭m7
A♭7
Fm7
B♭m7
G♭
E♭m
bout my dream man, my gen - tle he - man, the man for me, man, my
f delib. (move/string)
sim.

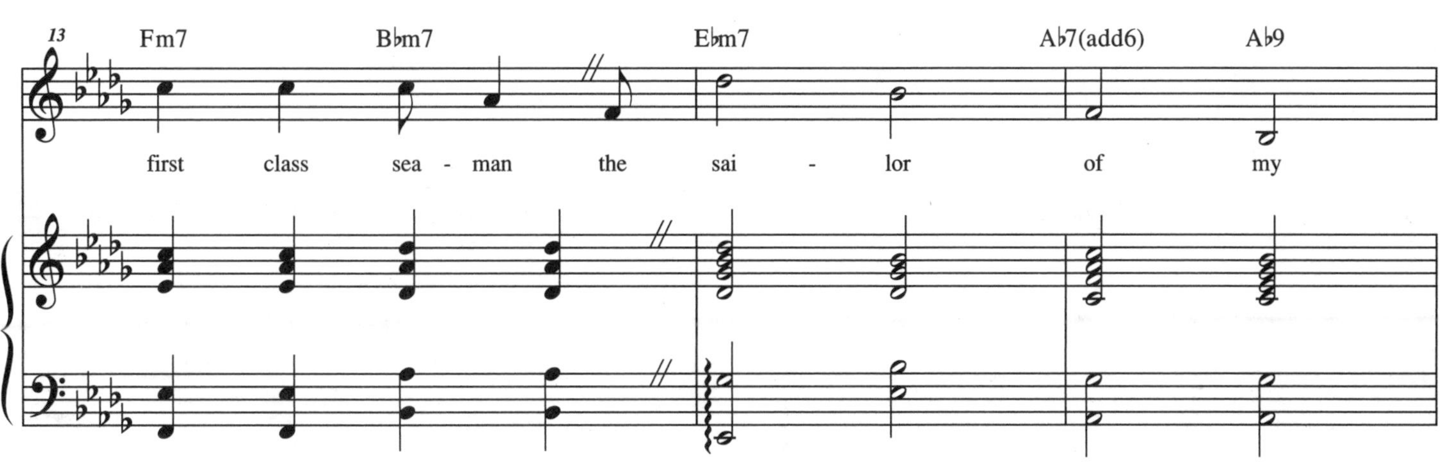
13
Fm7
B♭m7
E♭m7
A♭7(add6)
A♭9
first class sea - man the sai - lor of my

16
D♭
C
D♭
dreams.
8va

SHOW ME
(from "My Fair Lady")

Words by
ALAN JAY LERNER

Music by
FREDERICK LOEWE

CD/TRACK 2/31

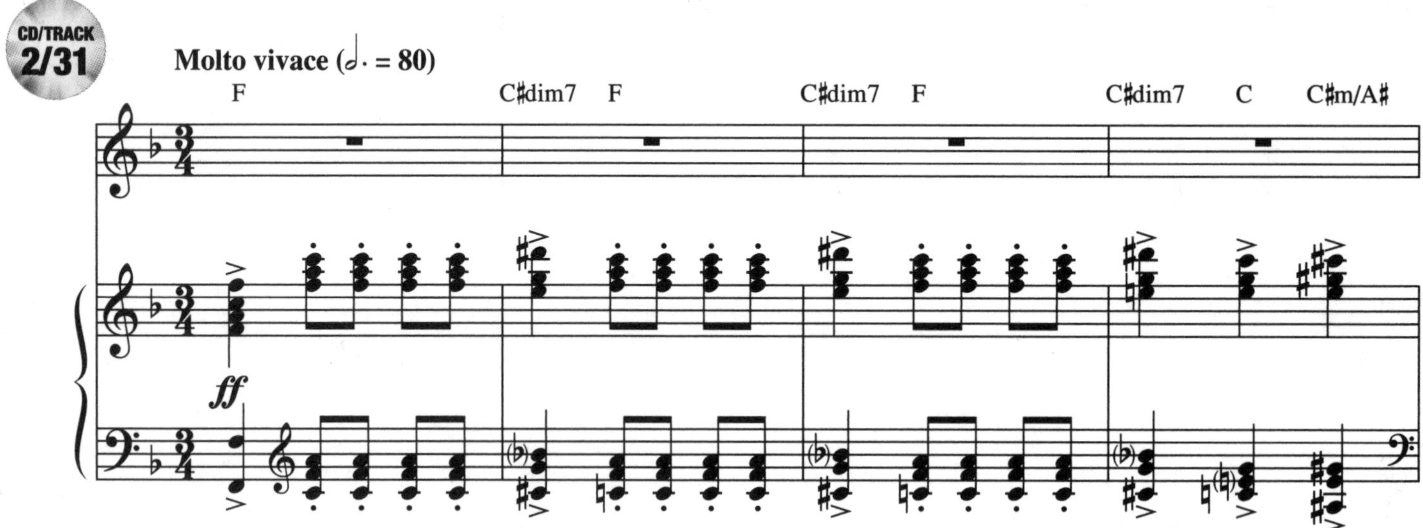

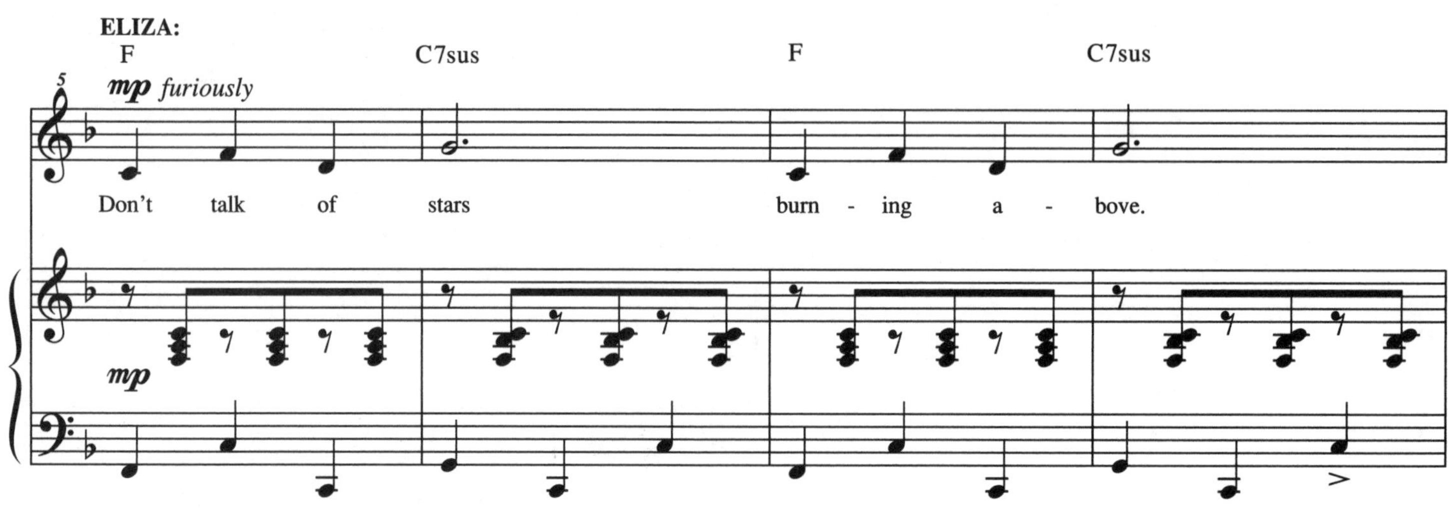

13
A♭
E♭7sus
A♭
E♭7sus
Tell me no dreams filled with de - sire.
mp
17
A♭
E♭7sus
A♭
mf
If you're on fire, show me!
mf
Optional start
21
C7
G7(♭9)
Here we are to - geth - er in the mid - dle of the night! Don't talk of
25
C
G7(♭9)
C
spring! Just hold me tight!
f
8va

29
C7
C
G7(♭9)
An - y - one who's ev - er been in love - 'll tell you that this is no
sf
33
C
Ddim7
D♭7
C
ff
C♯dim7
C
C♯dim7
C
C♯m/A♯
time for a chat!
sf
ff
37
F
mf
C7sus
F
C7sus
Have - n't your lips longed for my touch?
mf
41
F
E♭6
D7
Don't say how much; show me!

45
Gm
Gm7(♭5)
F/C
D♭7
Show me!
Don't talk of love
49
F/C
D♭7
F/C
cresc.
G7(♭9 ♭5)
last - ing through time.
Make me no un - dy - ing vow.
54
F/C
C7sus
F/C
C7sus
Show
me
59
F
C♯dim7
F
C♯dim7
F/C
C♯m/A♯
F
now!

SHY

(from "Once Upon a Mattress")

Words by
MARSHALL BARER

Music by
MARY RODGERS

CD/TRACK 2/32

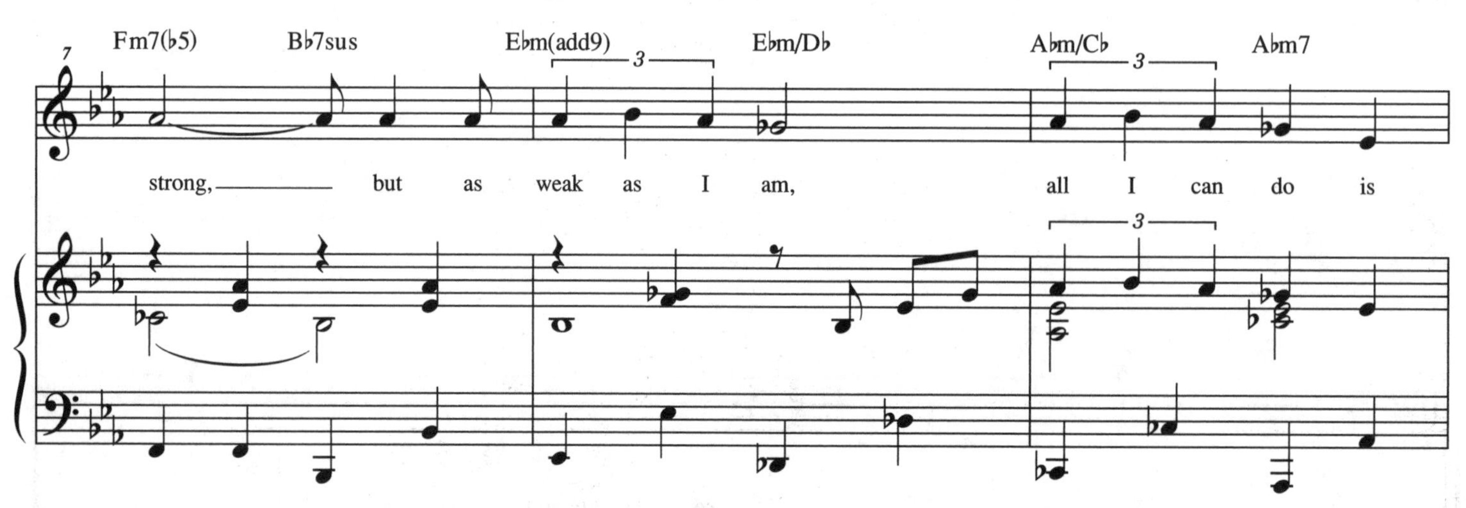

10
B♭9
E♭(add9)
Fm7
B♭7
try. God knows I try! though I'm fright - ened and
13
E♭(add9)
Fm7
B♭7
B♭m7/E♭
E♭13
shy; and de - spite the im - pres - sion I give, I con -
16
A♭
A♭m6
F7(♯11)
Fm7(♭5)/C♭
-fess that I'm liv - ing a lie! Be - cause I'm
19
E♭/B♭
E♭maj7/B♭
Fm7
B♭9
E♭(add9)
a tempo
ac - tual - ly ter - ri - bly ti - mid and hor - rib - ly shy.
a tempo

THE SIMPLE JOYS OF MAIDENHOOD

(from "Camelot")

Lyrics by
ALAN JAY LERNER

Music by
FREDERICK LOEWE

CD/TRACK 2/33

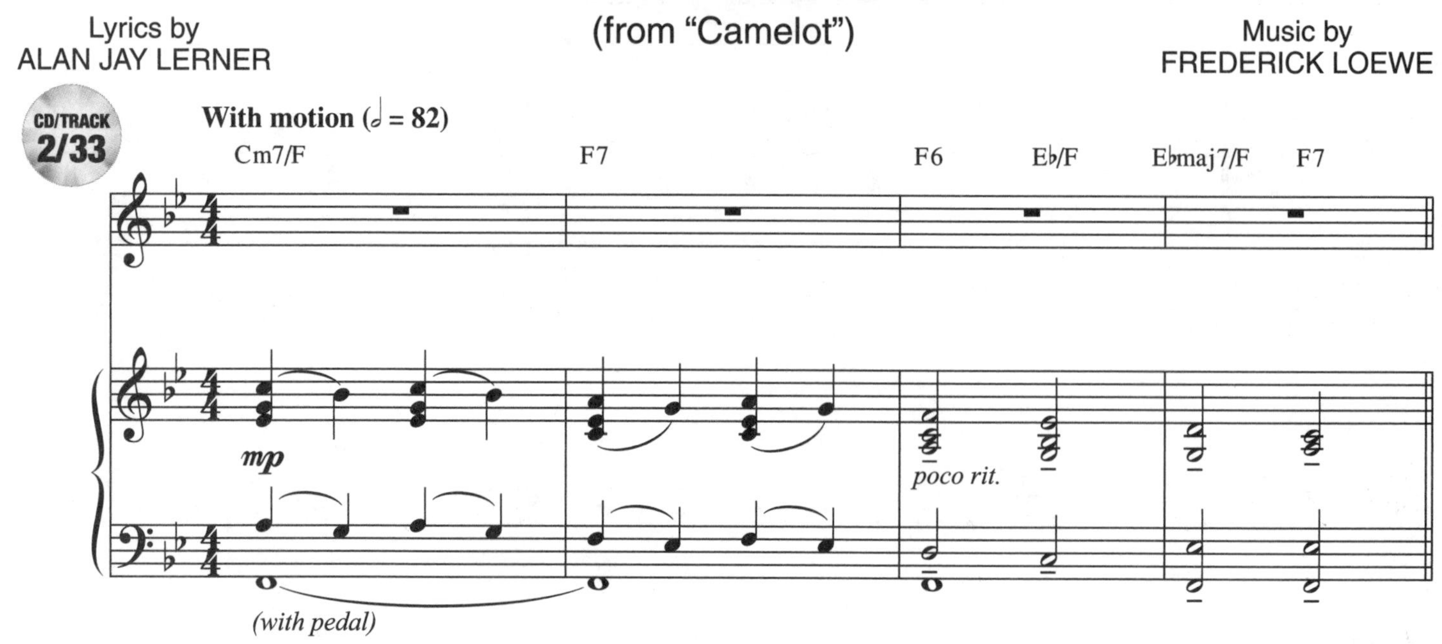

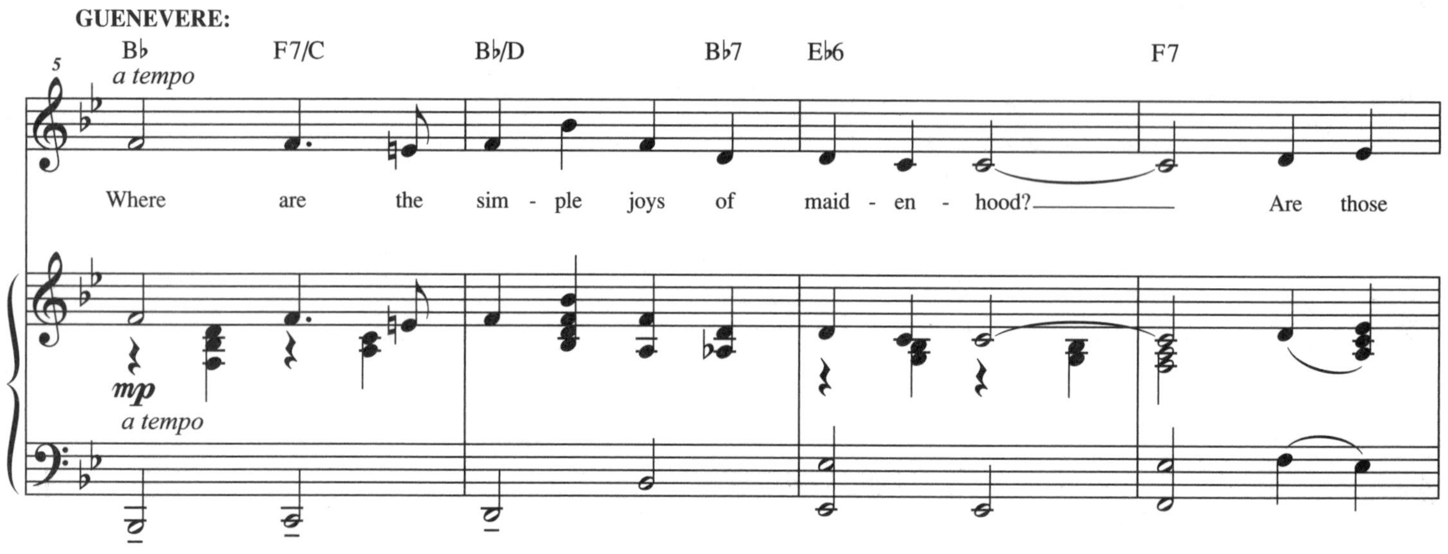

13
Bb/F D/F# Gm Dm7/F Eb6 Dm G+ Bb7/C Ab7/C
feud not be - gin for me? Shall kith not kill their kin for me? Oh,
17
Bb/F F7sus Bb/F Eb Bb/F F7 Bb/F C7 F7
rall.
where are the triv - ial joys...? Harm - less, con - viv - ial joys...?
rall.
21
Bb F7/C Bb/D Eb Ebm6 Bb/F F7
a tempo
poco rit.
Where are the sim - ple joys of maid - en -
a tempo
poco rit.
25
Bb Bb/F Eb Eb/G F7 Bb
mf poco più mosso
- hood?
mf poco più mosso
f

SOME THINGS ARE MEANT TO BE

(from "Little Women")

Lyrics by
MINDI DICKSTEIN

Music by
JASON HOWLAND

11
G(add9)
D/F#
C/E
Am7
meant to be: The clouds mov - ing fast and free. The sun on a
13
D7sus
D7
Gmaj7
C/D
D7sus
sil - ver sea. A sky that's bright and blue. And some things will
15
G(add9)
D/F#
C/E
Am7
nev - er end: The thrill of our mag - ic ride. The love that I
17
D7sus
D
G
G/F#
Em7
D
G(no3)
feel in - side for you.
rit.

SOMEONE TO WATCH OVER ME

(from "Oh, Kay!")

Music and Lyrics by
GEORGE GERSHWIN and IRA GERSHWIN

CD/TRACK 2/35

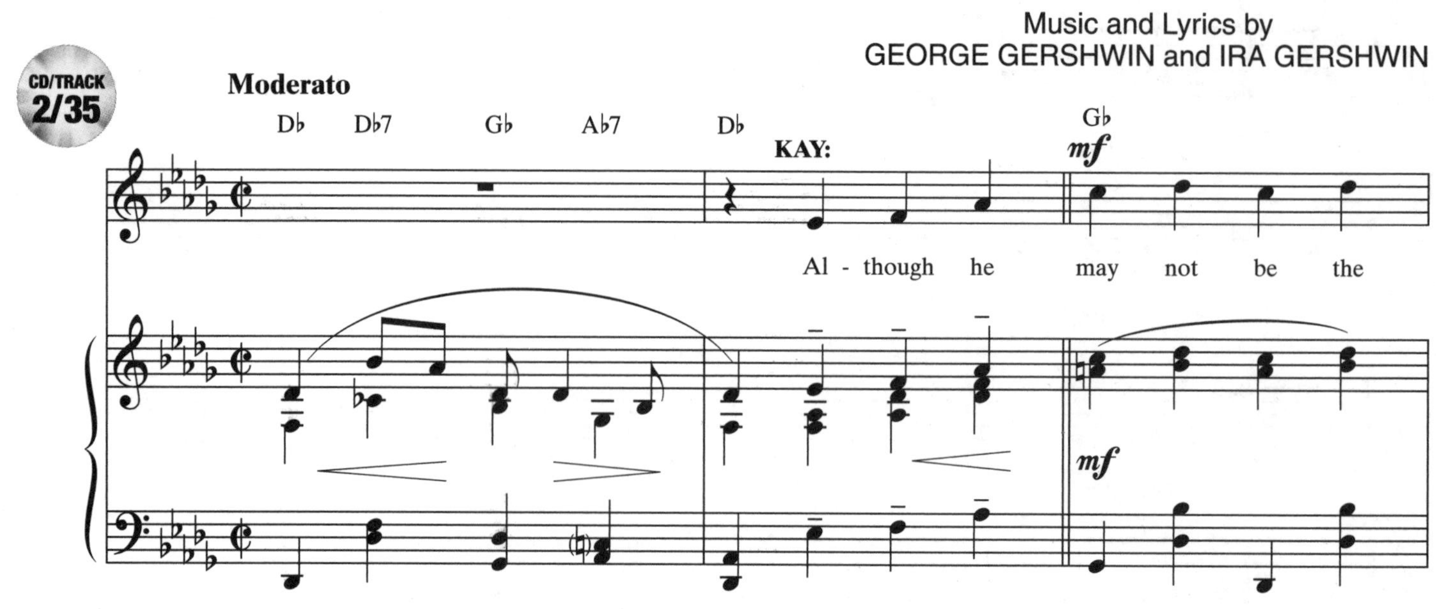

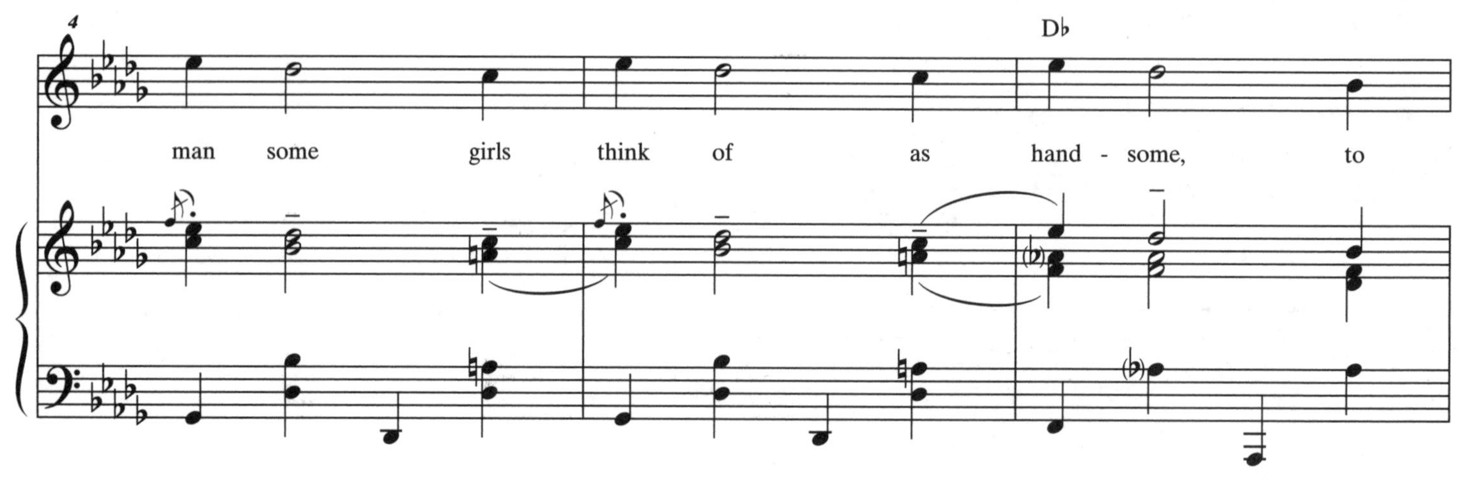

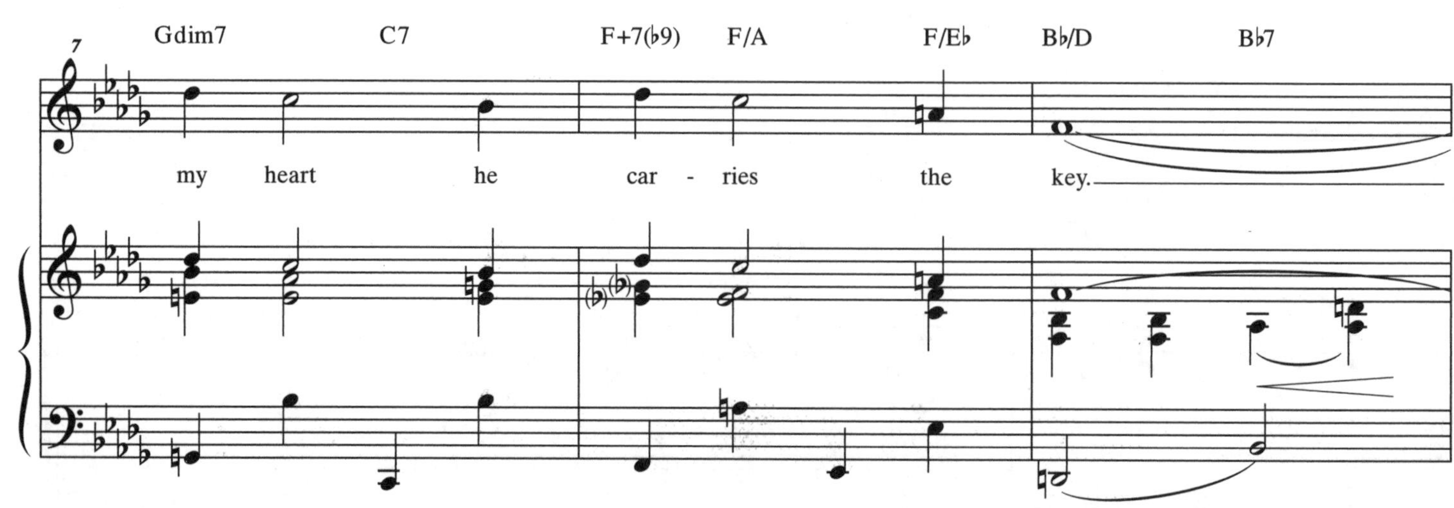

10
Eb7
Ab7
Db
Db7
Gb
Gbdim7
Won't you tell him please to put on some speed,
p

13
Db/F
Edim7
Ab7/Eb
Ddim7
Ebm
fol - low my lead,
oh, how I need
some - one to

16
Gm7(b5)
Gb/Ab
Ab7
Db
Db7
Gb
Gbm
Db
watch o - ver me.
mf

SOMEWHERE THAT'S GREEN

(from "Little Shop of Horrors")

Lyrics by
HOWARD ASHMAN

Music by
ALAN MENKEN

16
G/D
A7/C♯
A7
C/D
D7
C/D
D7
F/G
G7
- dy as the sun sets in the west. A pic - ture out of
20
F/G
G7
F/C
C
C♯m7(♭5)
Em/C♯
freely
Bet-ter Homes and Gar-dens mag - a - zine. Far from Skid
with pedal
24
G/D
D7sus
Row, I dream we'll go some - where that's
8va
with pedal
28
G
a tempo
C/G
D/G
G
C/G
D/G
G
C/G
D/G
G
green.
a tempo
pp

THE STORY GOES ON

(from "Baby")

Words by
RICHARD MALTBY, JR.

Music by
DAVID SHIRE

13 Fm6
C/E
Am7
Dm7
cresc.
what's to be. And thus it is our sto - ry
cresc.
16 F/G G Am/G F/G
C(add9)
ff
B♭/C
goes on and on and
ff
19 C(add9)
B♭/C
C(add9)
on and on and on.
22
molto rit.

SUDDENLY SEYMOUR

(from "Little Shop of Horrors")

Lyrics by
HOWARD ASHMAN

Music by
ALAN MENKEN

CD/TRACK 2/38

Bright pop ballad (♩ = 92)

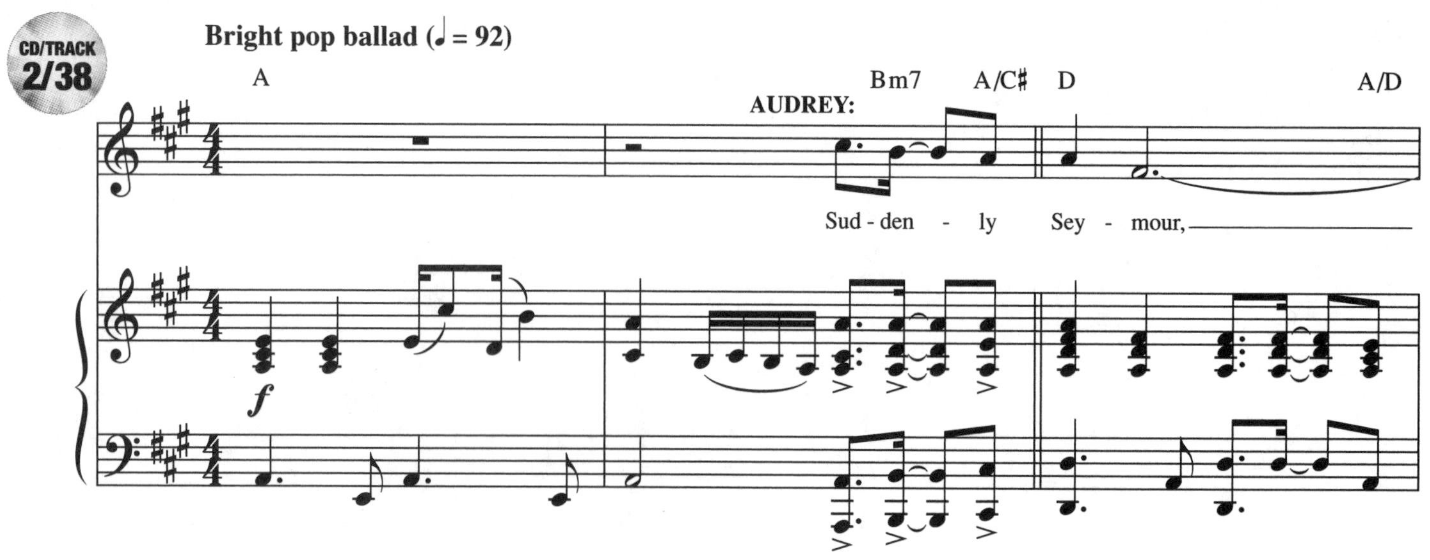

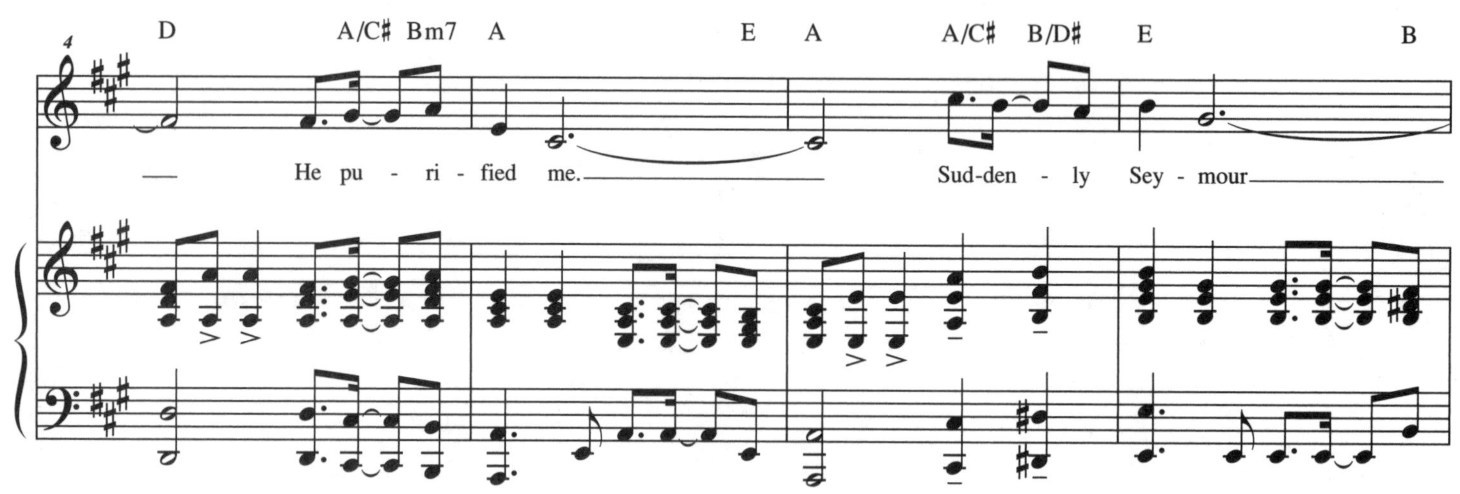

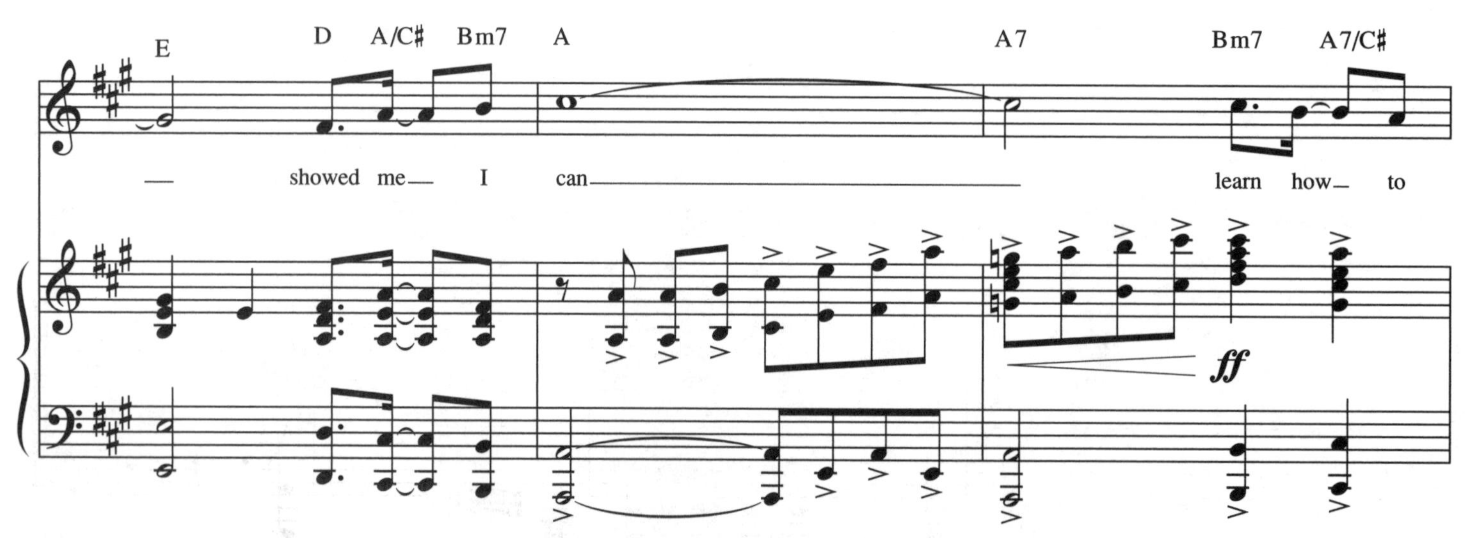

D A D B7/D♯ A/E Fdim7 F♯m7 F♯m7/E
be more the girl that's in - side me. With sweet un - der -
A/B B7 Dm
stand - ing, With sweet un - der - stand - ing,
A/E Esus
With sweet un - der - stand - ing, Sey - mour's my
A B/A Dm/A A
man.
sfz

SUPERBOY AND THE INVISIBLE GIRL

(from "Next to Normal")

Lyrics by
BRIAN YORKEY

Music by
TOM KITT

D5
C5/D
D5
Su - per-boy and the in - vi - si - ble girl…
Son of steel and daugh - ter of
f
A5/D
G
D
D(add9) D
air.
He's a he - ro, a lov-er, a prince, she's not there…
G
D
D(add9) D
G
She's not there…
She's not
D
D(add9) D
G
rit.
D
there…
She's not there.
ff

TAKE ME TO THE WORLD

(from "Evening Primrose")

Words and Music by
STEPHEN SONDHEIM

CD/TRACK 2/40

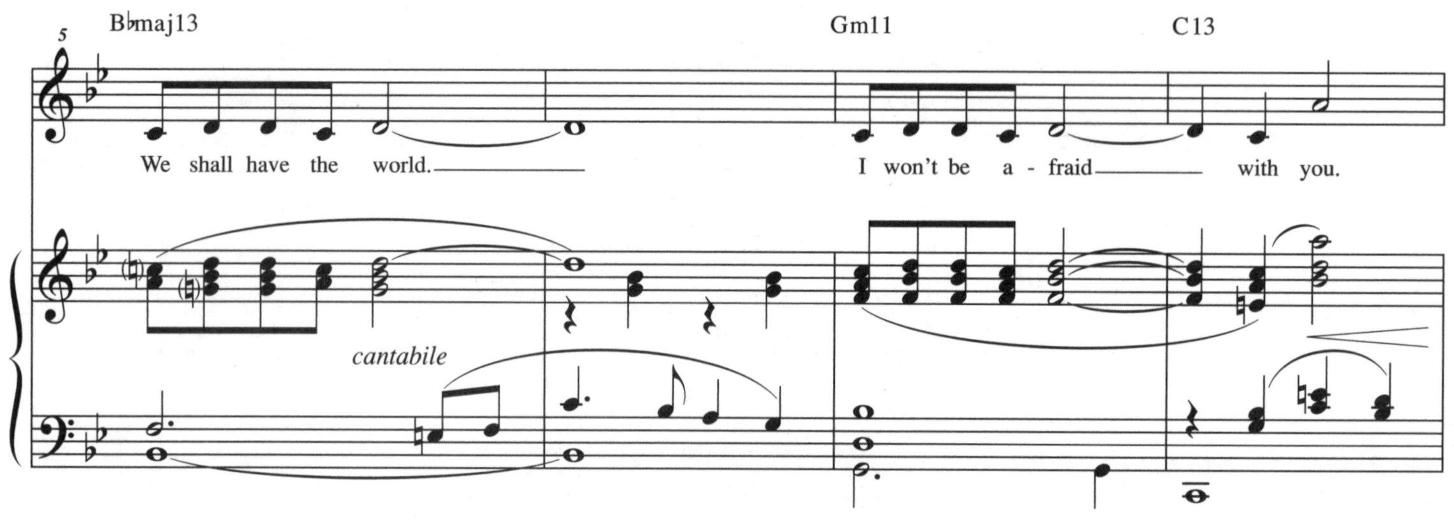

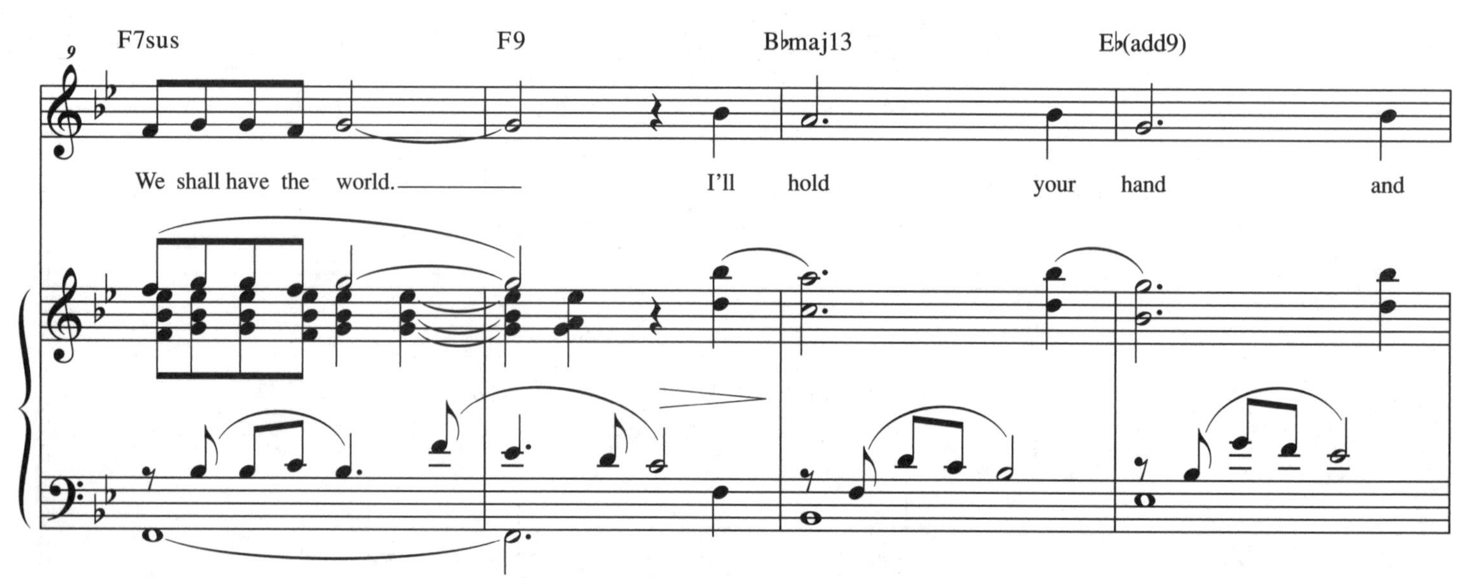

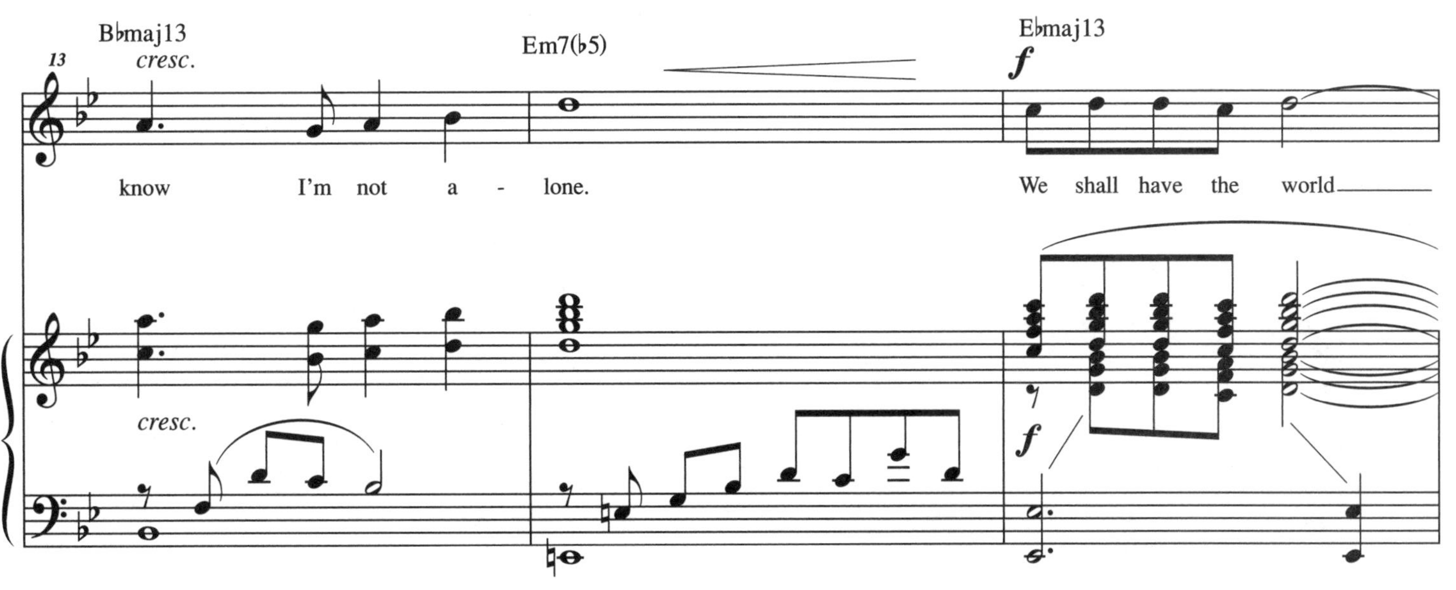
B♭maj13
13
cresc.
Em7(♭5)
E♭maj13
f
know I'm not a - lone.
We shall have the world
cresc.
f

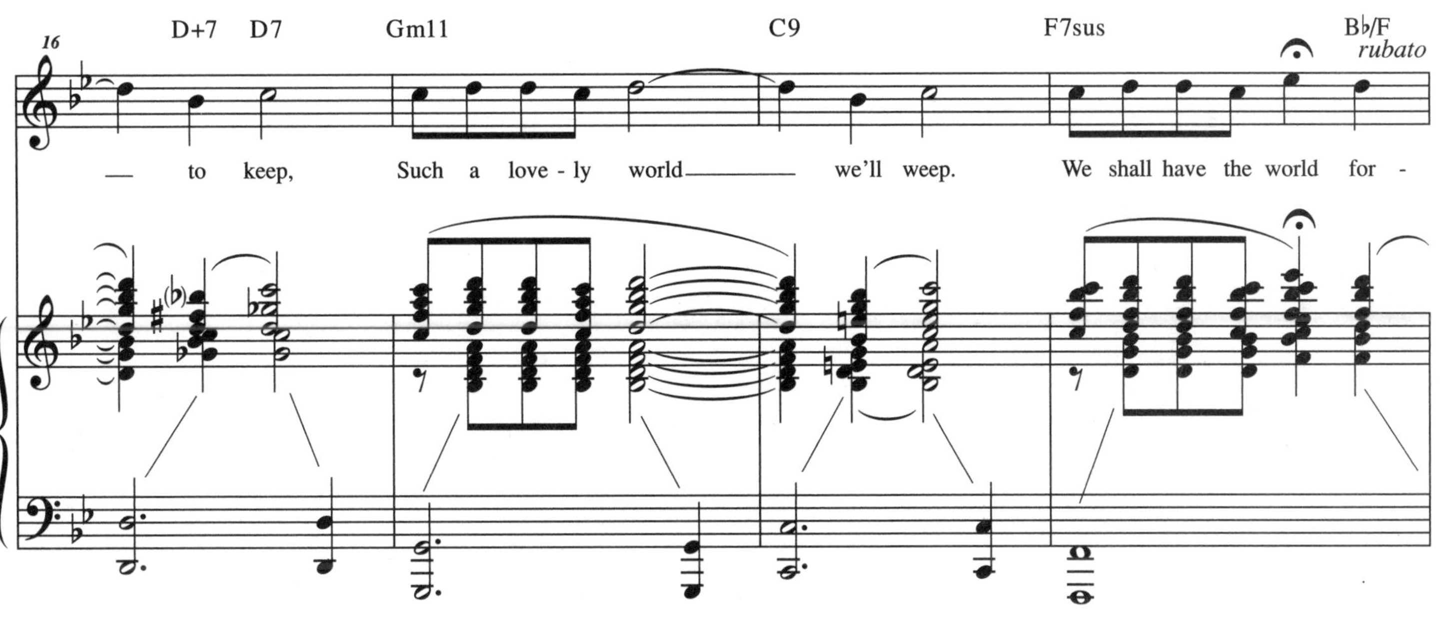
16
D+7 D7
Gm11
C9
F7sus
B♭/F
rubato
— to keep,
Such a love - ly world
we'll weep.
We shall have the world for -

20
G♭/A♭ B♭m7
Gm/F F9
B♭(add9)
p a tempo
rall.
- ev - er for our
own.
a tempo
colla voce
p
dim. poco a poco
rall.
pp

THERE WON'T BE TRUMPETS
(from "Anyone Can Whistle")

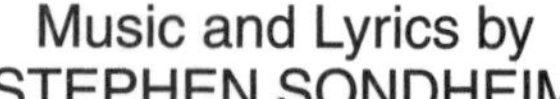

CD/TRACK 2/41

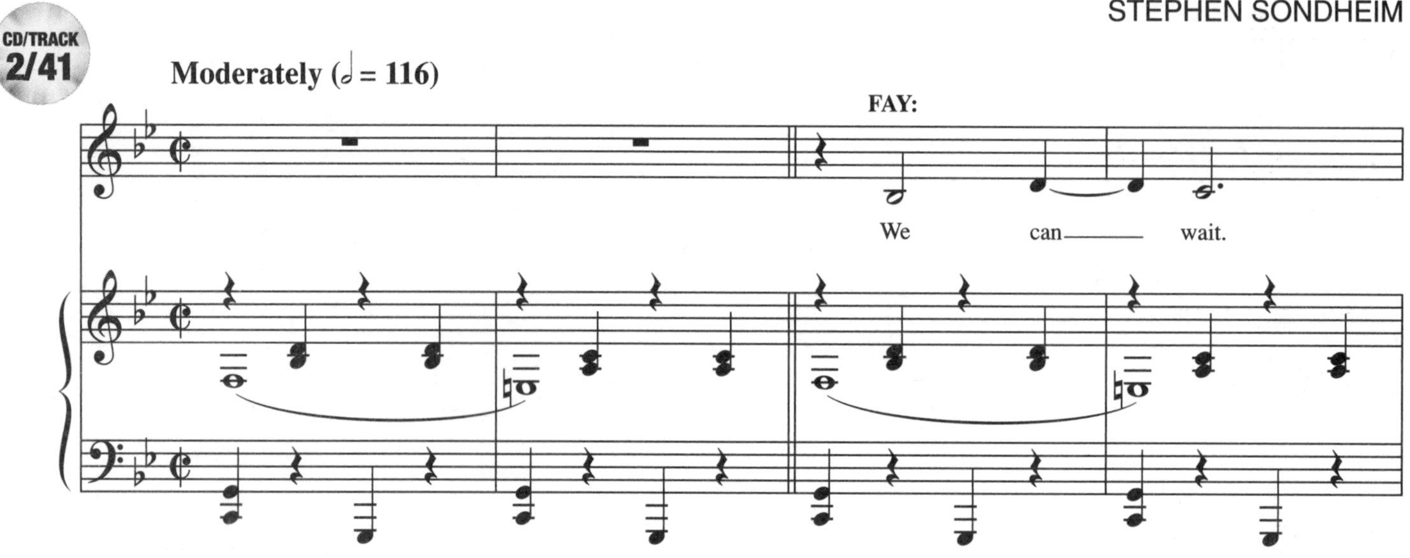

15
rall.
nick
of
time!
You
L.H.
rall.
19
Faster
won't
need
trum - pets!
There
3
23
are
no
trum - pets!
3
27
Who
needs
trum - pets?

THIS IS ALL VERY NEW TO ME

(from "Plain And Fancy")

Lyrics by
ARNOLD HORWITT

Music by
ALBERT HAGUE

24
Ebm(maj7)
Ebm7
Ab+
Cb/Db
Db7
Gbmaj7
And I'm knock - ing on wood. What to
30
Gbm6
Fm7
Edim7
Ebm7
Ab7
Fm7(b5)
do? What to say? How to make it go on this
36
Bb7
Gbmaj7
Gbm6
Fm7
Edim7
Ebm7
rit.
Ab7
way? Wish that I un - der - stood 'Cause it
rit.
42
Gb/Ab
Ab9
Ab7(b9)
Dbmaj9
Gb6/Bb
Dbmaj9
Gb6/Bb
Dbmaj9
f
feels oh so good
f

TIMES LIKE THIS

(from "Lucky Stiff")

Lyrics by
LYNN AHRENS

Music by
STEPHEN FLAHERTY

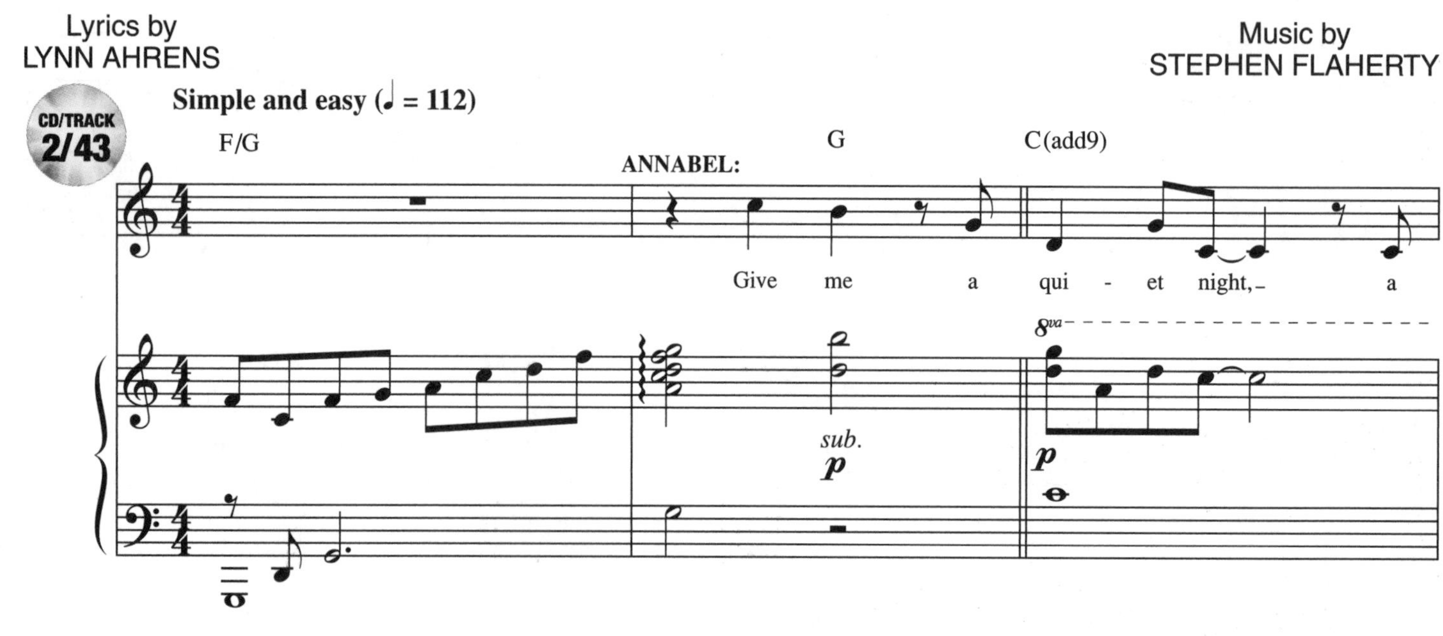

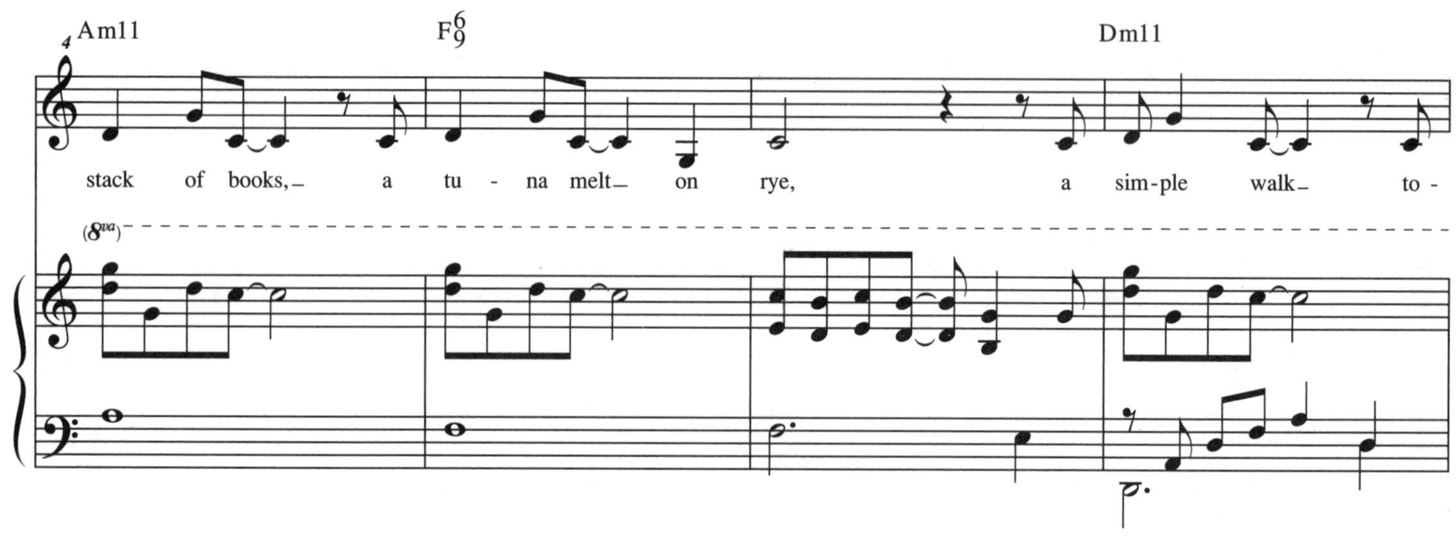

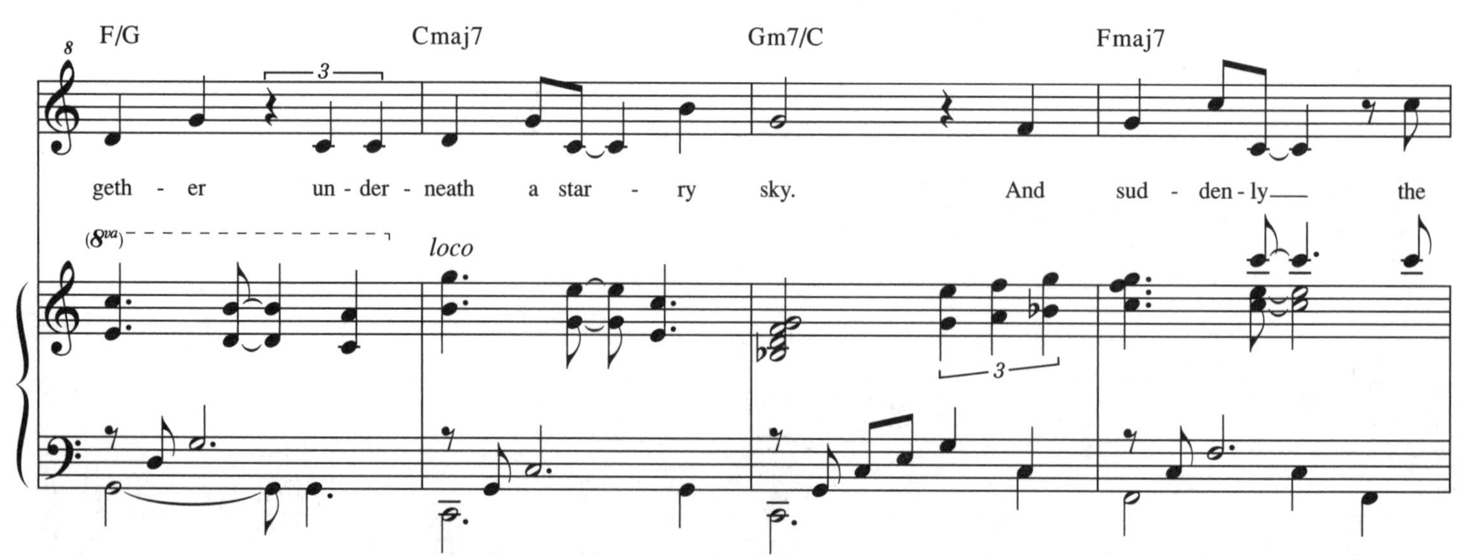

12
E7(♯9) /G♯ Am Gm11 C F(add9)
night is some - thing rare, and all be - cause - there's
16
E7(♯9) /G♯ Am7 F♯m7(♭5) F6/9
some - one spe - cial there who's gaz - ing at the
8va
mf
20
Em7 Am C/G Dm11 C/E
poco a poco rit.
views, his head up - on your shoes, At times like this I
poco a poco rit.
p
24
F6 F/G Slowly F6/9 F/G C
rit.
sure could use a dog.
pp
rit.
8va

THE TROLLEY SONG

(from "Meet Me in St. Louis")

Words and Music by
HUGH MARTIN and RALPH BLANE

CD/TRACK 2/44

Brightly (in 2) ($\text{half note} = 144$)

C6 ESTHER: C6

mf

"Clang, clang, clang," went the trol - ley,

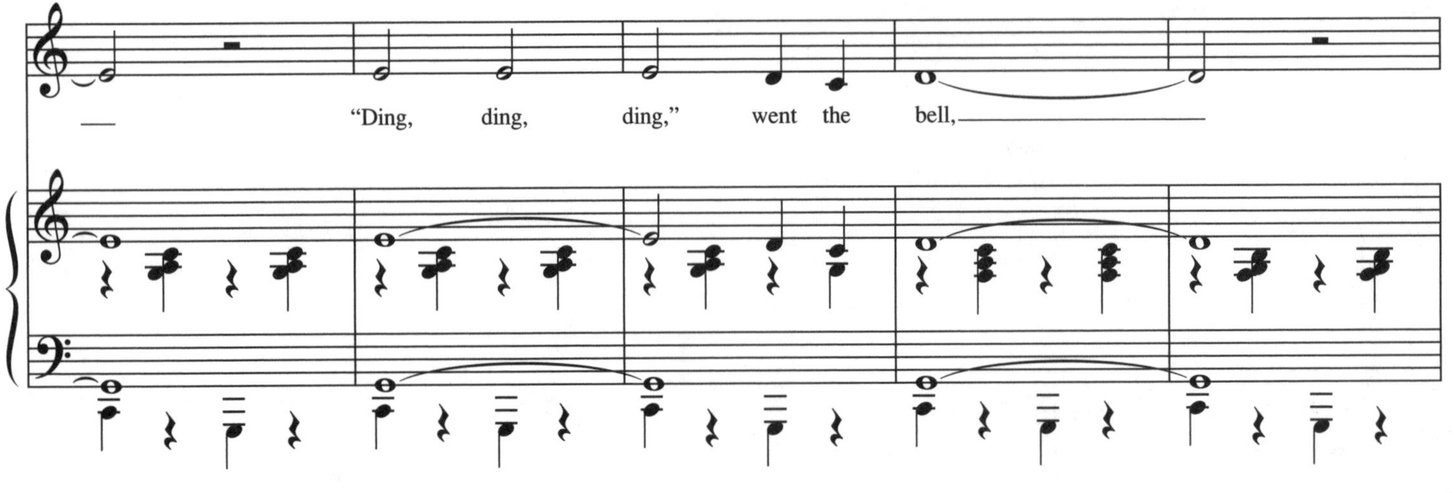

C6
Fm6
C6/E
E♭dim7
hold of his sleeve with my hand and as
Dm7
G7/D
A7/C♯
if it were planned, he stayed on with me.
Dm7
G7
Em7
A7(♭9)
F6
E7/G♯
Am
Am(maj7)
Am7
cresc.
And it was grand, just to stand with his hand hold-ing mine,
Dm7
G7sus
G7
C6
C6
to the end of the line.

WAITING FOR LIFE

(from "Once on This Island")

Lyrics by
LYNN AHRENS

Music by
STEPHEN FLAHERTY

CD/TRACK 2/45

Bright Caribbean feel

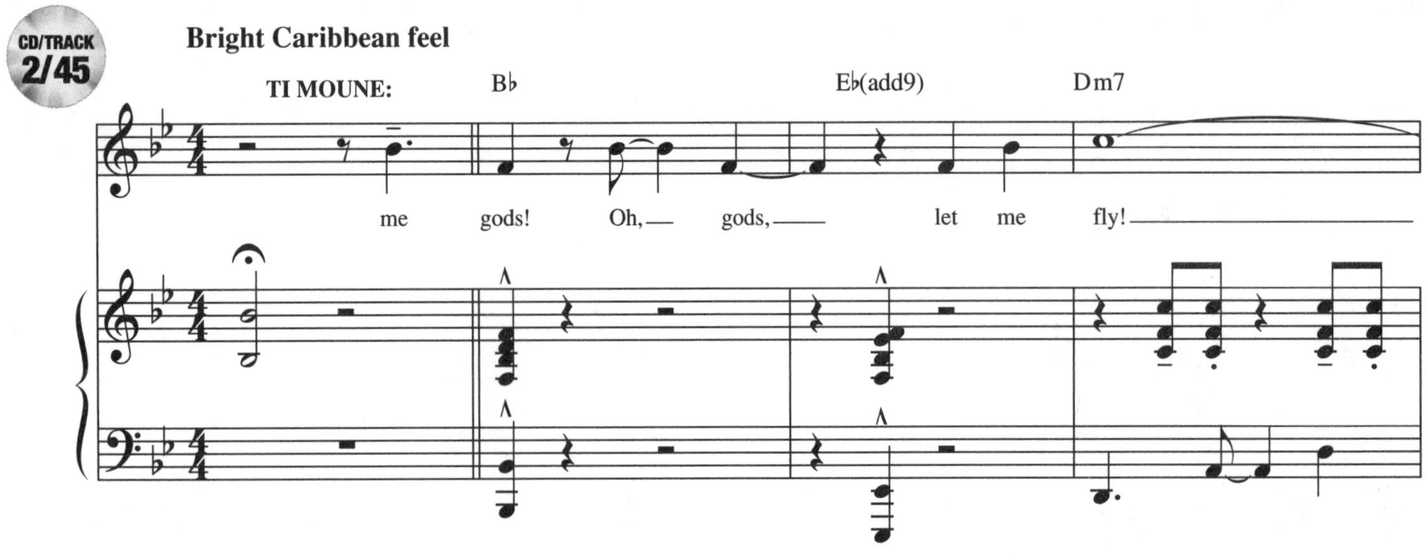

12
Dm7
Gm11
Cm11
B♭/D
why you get me to rise like a fish to the bait, then
16
E♭6/9
F7sus
tell me to wait. Well, I'm wait - ing,
8va
19
3
3
wait - ing for life to be -
sfz
(8va)
22
B♭
F7sus
E♭(add9)
N.C.
- gin!
sfz

WHEN I LOOK AT YOU
(from "The Scarlet Pimpernel")

Lyrics by
NAN KNIGHTON

Music by
FRANK WILDHORN

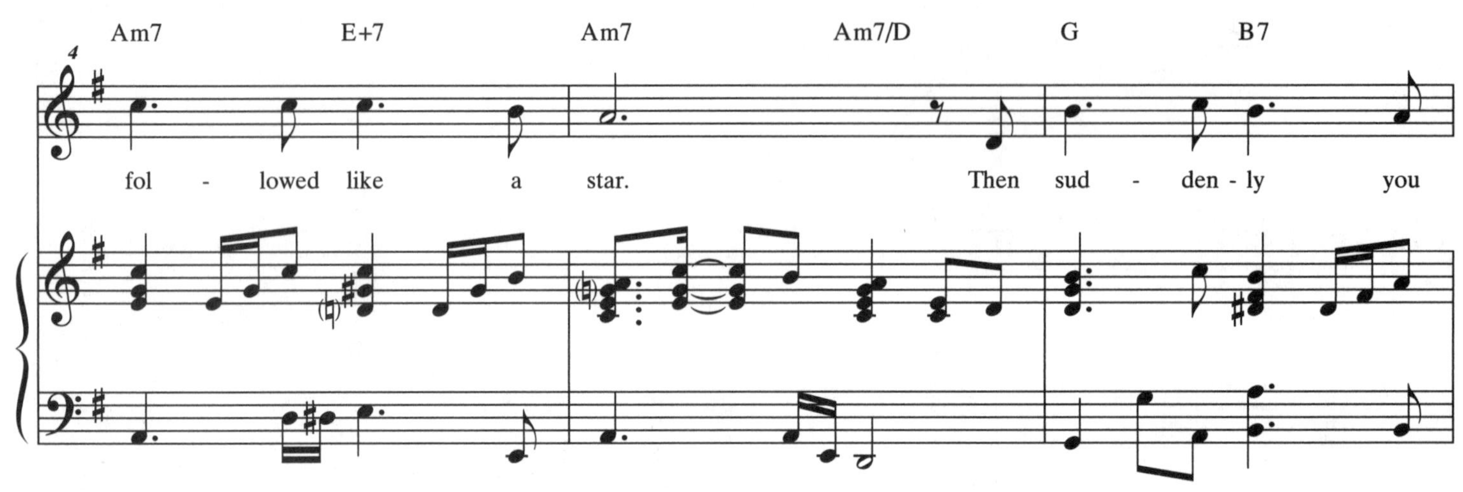

10
Cmaj7
B7sus
B7
Em7
Cm6
G/D
be that I nev - er real - ly knew you from the start? Did I cre - ate a dream? Was he a
13
Am7/D
G
G/B
Cmaj7
Am7(♭5)
freely
fan - ta - sy? E-ven a mem - o - ry is par - a - dise for all the fools like me. Now re -
16
G
Am7
Em7
A9
Am7
mem-ber-ing is all that I can do, be-cause I miss him so when I
19
C/D
G
Cm6
G(add9)
look at you.

WHISPERING
(from "Spring Awakening")

Lyrics by
STEVEN SATER

Music by
DUNCAN SHEIK

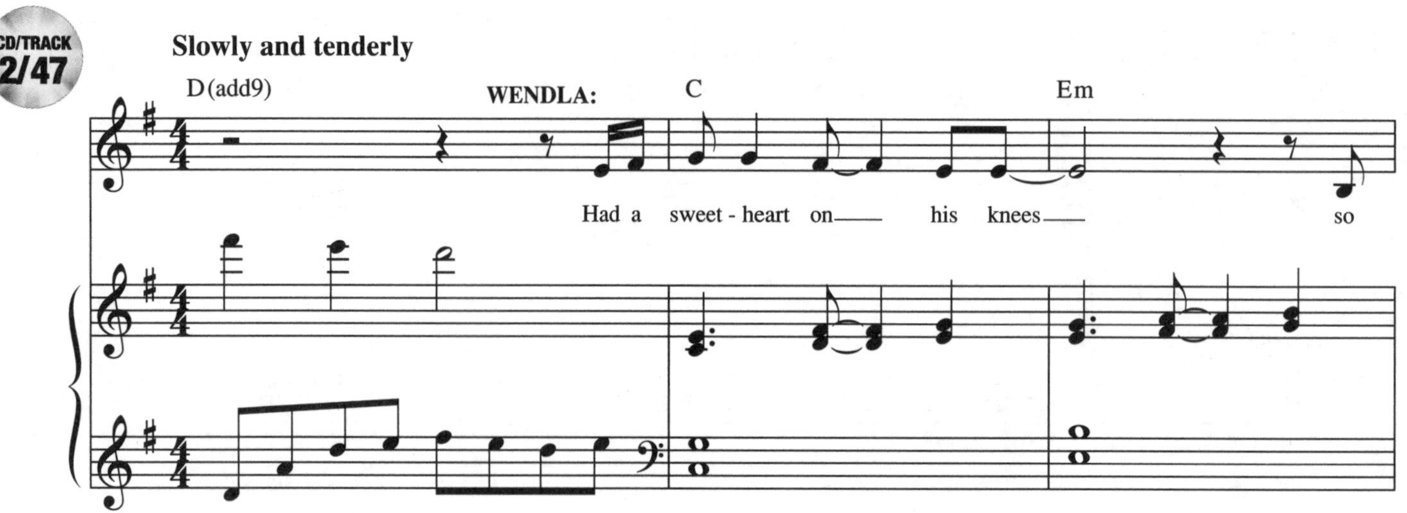

10
A
A11
13
Em7
A7/E
Cmaj7/E
3
Lis - ten - ing
for the hope,
for the new life,
16
Em(add9)
Em7
A7/E
some-thing beau - ti - ful,
a new chance.
Hear its
19
Cmaj7/E
D(add9)
Em
whis-per-ing
there a - gain.
rall.

WOULDN'T IT BE LOVERLY
(from "My Fair Lady")

Lyrics by
ALAN JAY LERNER

Music by
FREDERICK LOEWE

Gm7/C
C7
F
B♭
Gm7
C7
o - ver the win - dow - sill.
Some - one's head rest - in' on my knee;
F
G7
C7
F
C7/E
Cm6/E♭ D7
B♭m/D♭
Warm and ten - der as he can be;
Who takes good care of me. Oh,
F/C
Dm
Gm7
C7
F
C7
rall.
Would - n't It Be Lov - er - ly,
lov - er - ly,
rall.
F
B♭
F
lov - er - ly,
lov - er - ly,
lov - er - ly.

YOU TOOK ADVANTAGE OF ME

(from "Present Arms")

Words by
LORENZ HART

Music by
RICHARD RODGERS

Lilting (♩ = 96)

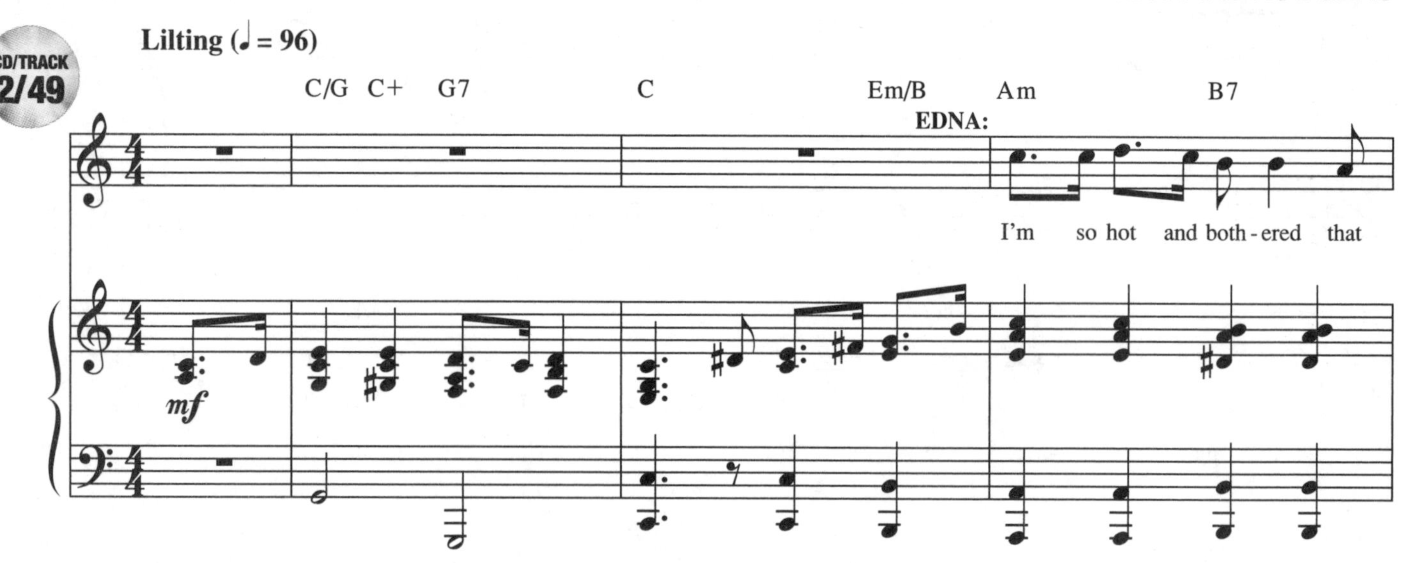

10
Em7
Dm7
G7
C
C♯dim
G7
near.
Here I am with all my bridg - es burned,

13
C/E
E♭dim
Dm7
G7
C/E
C7
just a babe in arms where you're con - cerned, so lock the doors and

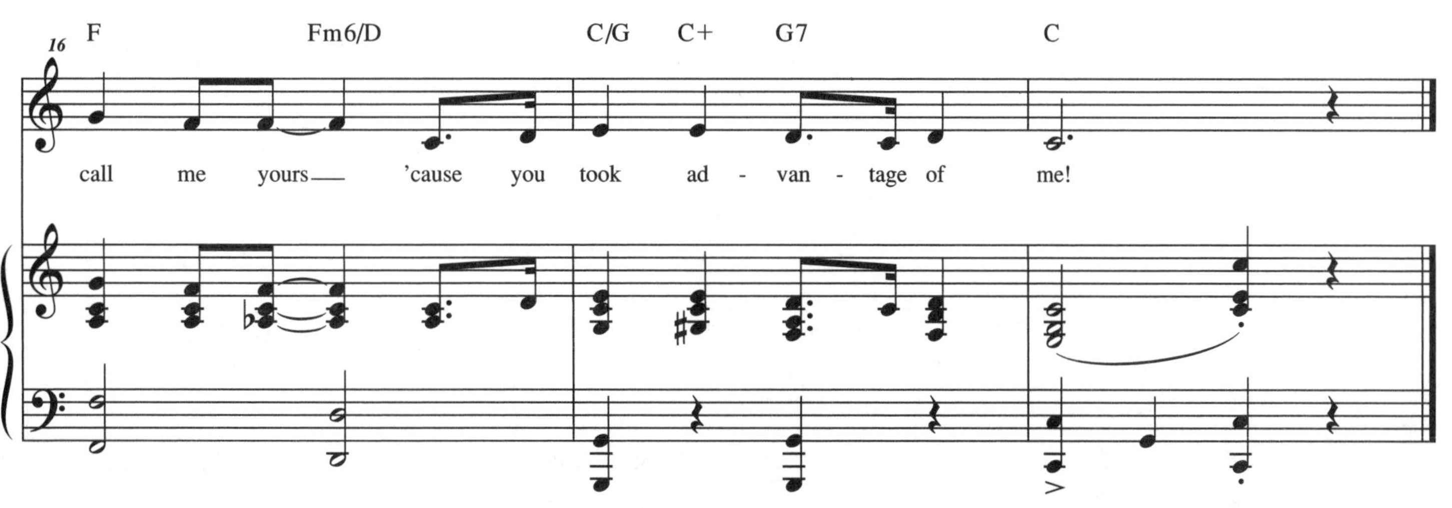
16
F
Fm6/D
C/G
C+
G7
C
call me yours 'cause you took ad - van - tage of me!

YOUR DADDY'S SON
(from "Ragtime")

Lyrics by
LYNN AHRENS

Music by
STEPHEN FLAHERTY

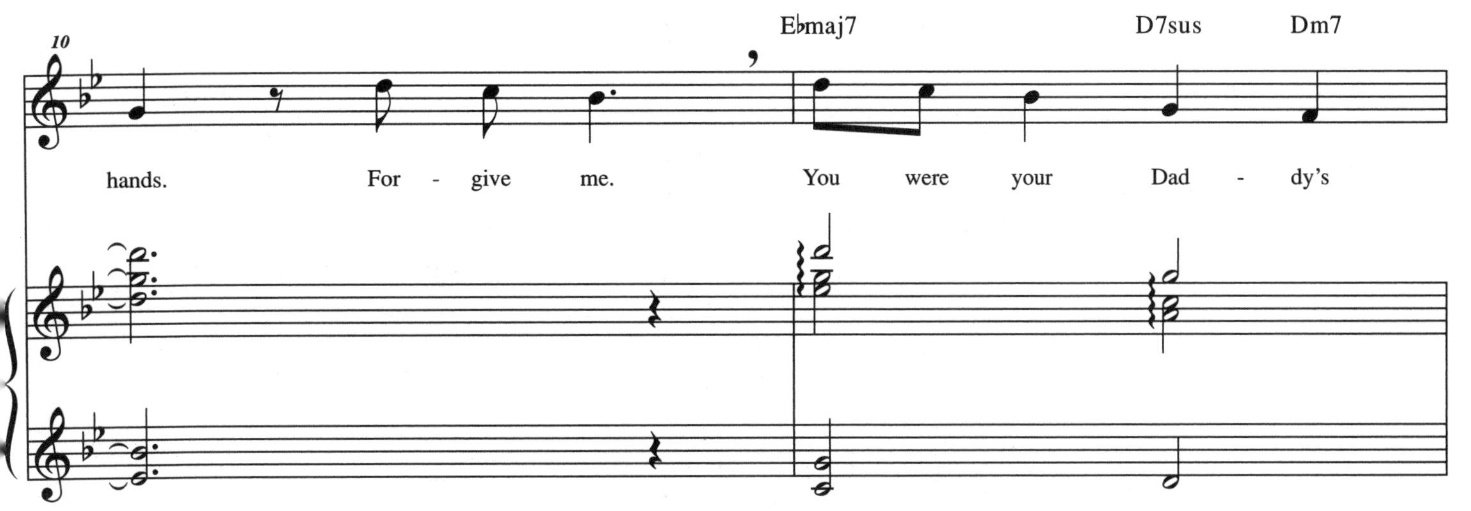
10
E♭maj7
D7sus
Dm7
hands. For - give me. You were your Dad - dy's

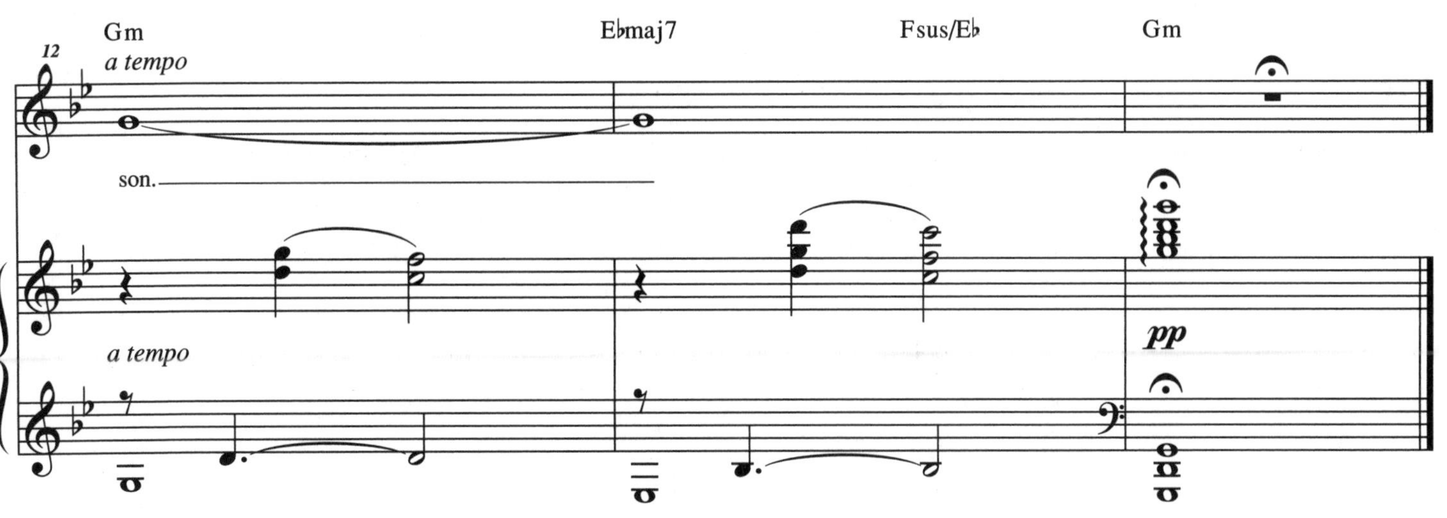
12
Gm
a tempo
E♭maj7
Fsus/E♭
Gm
son.
pp
a tempo